THE
KROHNICLES

Life of a Beatnik Boy

THE
KROHNICLES
Life of a Beatnik Boy

**The Story of a Very Unusual
American Family
Growing Up in the 1945 - 1965
'Beat' World**

PAT A. KROHN

The cover photo was first published in the the **Saturday Evening Post** on July 10,1950. The photo was taken by Frank Ross. It was captioned, *"Fisherman Bill Wagner and his family wouldn't swap their home afloat for a mainland mansion."*

ISBN: 978-1-468184-62-4

Preface

I truly cannot say enough to give appropriate credit and thanks to my beloved wife, Jessica Wicken, for her encouragement and suggestions along the way, and for typing and early editing of the manuscript. Also, I would especially like to thank our dear friend, Dr. Ellie Bloomfield, for spending countless hours poring over the first draft and giving me the benefit of her amazing editing skills to improve the telling of my story. Susan Gatchet Reese, from KUVO FM Radio at 89.3 in Denver, was very helpful as well, with her constructive criticism. Finally, I am so grateful to my friend Lynette McClain for shepherding this manuscript through the final process of becoming an actual book.

I am also very thankful to have been able to interview my parents from time to time, and to finish this story while they were still alive.

Disclaimer

Everyone in the book could write their own story of the same people and events and come up with a different version of the truth. That is the nature of the human experience. These are my memories, subject to my own subjectivity. Remembering things differently is okay.

Contents

1 The Krohnicles

Everybody has a story to tell about his or her life that is unique and unusual. However, in every society of people, most people tend to be, try to be, want to be (sometimes desperately so) like everybody else. Most people don't stop and think how really un-American that is. I mean this *is* the "land of the free and home of the brave," meaning, having the courage to be free enough to explore, discover, experiment, create, discuss, live, love and pursue happiness, and try to be responsible to others' freedom and need to pursue those things and more, i.e. that which is interesting.

To a child that sort of abstract thinking is beyond comprehension. Children just do it naturally and are responsible to the best they know how. The only limit a child knows is what he or she has learned. That's me.

My parents were what used to be called non-conformists. My father, Peter, was a carpenter and boat builder, and an artist (an abstract painter). Actually, his carpentry (fine woodwork) and boat building was an extension or further expression of his artistry. As far back as I can remember, he was self-employed at these endeavors except for one year working for Ringling Art Museum and a few months as Art Director for the Ringling Circus Float in Sarasota, Florida. My mother was a poet. Besides being a loving and attentive mother, she always tried to be a partner in my father's work. She also did waitress work now and then, when I was 8 or 9, and a month or two when I was 12.

All the time I grew up we never had a telephone, TV, radio or a car. We were different and different on purpose. We were spared the pollution and corruption of being like everybody else. We were free from the slavery of those things. Life was our own unique version of Thoreau's Walden Pond experience. There were times when the whole family could be seen (mom, dad and three boys) going down the road on five bicycles.

As long as I can remember we never stayed anywhere more than a year or two. Home was wherever we were, either an earthly dwelling or on a boat. Jean, my mother, prided herself on being able to set up house in any setting and make the rest of us feel at home and comfortable. Whenever we moved, we each had a standard U.S. Navy sea bag and left our home just the way she set it up, in consideration of whoever might want to live there next. In this context or life style, many wonderful, interesting, adventurous things occurred, and many interesting people of all kinds came in and out of our lives.

Life is a journey of many destinations. Every twenty-four hours we circumnavigate our own individual world. Sometimes it can be a rich experience to reflect and trace your steps back to the beginning of what you call life, and recreate the events that grow into a story that at times is more fascinating than fiction, and at other times may uncover insights into the present. There are more ways of doing things than there are stars in the sky. This story is about how one family found their way.

2 Peter

My father, Peter Krohn, was born to Virginia
Warren, a rebellious, New York City intellectual,
Sorbonne-educated debutante, and Russell
Krohn, a Finnish bohemian living in Greenwich
Village. He was a painter (evidently the Krohn
name is famous in Finland for gracing artists,
poets, and other such creativists). However,
he disappeared when Peter was two years old,
never to be heard from again. As destiny would
have it, Virginia fell in love with John Wagner,
a writer and journalist for the New York Times
who then became the public relations man for
mayors LaGuardia and O'Dwyer. Evidently he
was well to do because they raised Peter and two
other sons named Mike and Pat in a nice home
with servants on Gramercy Park, possibly to the
chagrin of Virginia's family who had disowned
her when she took up with "that bohemian
painter" (Victorian values were a real hang-up in
the 1920s New York).

The Warren family was in the Mayflower
Society owing to a lineage that went back to
Sir Peter Warren (Peter's namesake), the first
English Governor in the late 1600's, returning

to England in the early 1700's after having a
mansion on what is now Manhattan Island
where there is still a street with his name. He also
had a large plantation in upstate New York called
the Warren Farm. He had won some important
battles against the French as an admiral of a
small fleet, which sealed the sovereignty of what
is now the East Coast of the United States, for
which he was awarded the governorship and
one third of the booty. That amounted to quite
a lot. He would bring his ship into a harbor,
pull down the Union Jack, and the Spanish and
French would enter thinking it unprotected
and then lose their ships. Sir Peter then took his
spoils and invested in the English Stock Market
and became, according to many, the richest man
in England at the time.

So Virginia and her son Peter were saved from
their terrible plight by love and a very gracious
noble and gentle man of whom my father always
expressed nothing but the fondest and best
regards, a good honest and as fair a man as there
could be, who would give a friend the shirt off
his back, values which Peter kept and taught to
us boys.

When Peter was six he came down with
a six-month case of dysentery, which nearly
killed him. He learned physical fitness during

rehabilitation and later went on to be the captain of the high school gym team and also excelled at track and cycling. He built his own bike from parts from four different countries that made the best of certain parts. He also was accepted at the prestigious Peter Stuyvesant High School because he was very good at math. Peter had a job at the bowling alley setting up pins. It must have been there that he became part of a gang. He stood out among them as the honest looking one, so they called him "Honest Bill", which suited him because he liked a radio program called "Just Plain Bill" so he would say, "Just call me Bill."

3 Peter and Jean

By this time Peter had already met Jean. When he was 15 and she was 13 he saw her on a swing, her pretty brown hair and sweet face, perfect young body. He walked up to her, grabbing the swing by the chains, looked into her deep dark brown eyes and said "Solid." Standing over her like that, looking down into her young developing voluptuous breasts with penetrating desire, he took her breath away. Peter was an incredibly handsome young man with his somewhere between Peter O'Toole and Fred Astaire features, blue, blue eyes, flowing blond hair and perfect gymnast's physique. They became lovers.

Jean

The quintessential mother,
Homemaker,
Source of nurture
The music to inspire Peter
The music of Peter and Jean
Primitive Spirit
Ancient Soul
Heavenly Dancer
Her children felt cared for
Not worried about.
The earth to Peter's Sea
She's something good
Out of nothing
And makes things that way
Simplicity personified
Remembering who you are
When it's important
Making you more
Applauding life
Jean loves to laugh
The what to Peter's who
The who to Peter's what.

Jean was from a very Catholic, French, German, Irish, Swiss, Italian background. Her father was an Italian named Joe Pescia, whose great grandfather was the son of the Count of Pescia in Italy, who came to America in the 1860's having run away with the Nubian maid, hence the African blood in our family, although not noticeable physically. The rest of the European mix is best described as a serendipitous cacophony of exotically attracted lovers. Jean was an interesting mixture of someone who sings, dances, i.e. liked to perform, was very good at academics, and devoted to her family and religion. She was a traditional girl with an adventurous spirit and a mind eager to learn. Jean's family did not approve of Peter and called him a "domineering Dutchman."

4 The War Years

In 1940 Peter got into trouble with his friends and was given the choice of going to reform school or going into the service. Peter had always been fond of the idea of being a sailor and going to sea, even stealing a boat with a friend, and on another occasion stowing away with a boat owner who had befriended him. Even though he was only 17, he got his father's permission to join the Navy, just before World War II was declared. Because of his keen math skills he became a navigator, and because of his gymnastic skills, he taught the officers how to work out on the high bars. Peter's war experiences were terrifying and something he never wanted to talk about. One time, when he was on leave, which he could have sold for $200, an officer gave the wrong coordinates when aiming a very large gun and blew out the whole section of the ship where my father was usually assigned, killing all of his friends. Another time, Peter was assigned to an escort boat that was a 100-foot yacht donated by Gloria Vanderbilt, one of many yachts that had been donated by wealthy people for the war effort. This one was exceptionally beautiful in nautical design with Honduras mahogany hardwood trim especially in the interior. It had a state-of-the-art record player much enjoyed by the crew. The two masts were removed and replaced by a gunnery platform with two 240-caliber machine guns. It had a 120 horsepower, six-cylinder diesel engine which enabled the boat to do ten knots. One of Peter's jobs was to assist the navigator who was frequently drunk.

On one such occasion Peter had to take over and position the boat over a German sub beneath them to drop depth charges on the sub. He remembers hearing their last words with each other and the human effects that floated up afterwards. It was a horrible war (what war isn't?) and he served in every arena including the Philippines and Murmansk Bay, in the North Sea where, according to my father, the Germans had the most feared Navy with the best and fastest ships in the world at that time.

Jean was in the hospital when he came home on leave and he shook her bed because he shook uncontrollably. He must have been on a birthday furlough in 1944, because my big brother Mike was born November 10 and Peter's birthday was February 19, the same as mine.

5 Home at Last

When the war was over Peter came home to Jean and Mike to start a new life. Through family connections he got a good job working for the New York City Parks Department as a cabinetmaker. He started as an apprentice and learned fine carpentry from a group of Italian cabinet workers that the Parks Department was lucky to have. Peter was assigned to work with an old master craftsman who taught him many ancient techniques.

The War was over and spirits were high everywhere, especially in New York. My big brother Mike was still an infant. Peter and Jean would leave him at home with grandma and Aunts Carol and June while they would go out dancing. Everybody was wailing and swinging to the "jitterbug, "jump swing" and Afro-Cuban music.

6 Sing and Dance

Singing, Dancing,
Always Romancing
In 1945 New York City,
The street corner works just fine
The lamppost's a swinging prop,
Skip that raindrop
The sun is shining,
In two young hearts life with lots of pop
Lots of late night lingering
Don't let the magic stop
Rhythms and melodies fill the air
This kind of fun can start anywhere
It will always be there
In between the wondering
Swing, jump, bebop,
Afro Cuban Jazz
There they go Jitterbugging,
Lots of hugging
Always kissing, never missing
The Key Notes,
Love in Crazy Time
Forget the rhyme
It's all like that, no right or wrong
Living is a song a beautiful Thing

No one knows How –
It just keeps happening
Everything is now
A little twinkle, a little wrinkle, A laugh
The sound before the sound
Is always ringing,
Always singing something new
Here, now, just around the corner
Knowing that love is such a friend
Like Sun, Moon, Stars,
There is no end
There is no doubt;
There is just a going on
Fear is an unworthy foe;
Life is too good to wait for nothing
Peter and Jean,
Loving to do what they love.

The art world was excited about colorful
new ways of expressing form and dimension,
textures with unpredictable kinds of beauty
and feelings, defined by the artists' use of
many mediums, inspired by music and visions;
spontaneous – personal, reflecting any number
of experiential, serendipitous, visually insightful,
even minimalist concepts inspired by Oriental
art or "primitive" art, or even beyond concepts
expressible in words. A brave new world certainly

encompassing much more than Aldous Huxley's *Brave New World*, as prophetic and significant as that was to their generation. A new kind of freedom, rooted in their forefathers' visions was taking place, and was forcing its way into their own young lives, driving their own adventure in life.

Naturally attracted to the bohemian spirit prevailing in the world of music, art, writing and related endeavors, (Jean was becoming a poet and writer), they wanted a real life for themselves and their children rather than one defined by Society. Already becoming nonconformists, they decided to move away from family influences that tended to drag them into a world they were not interested in.

One day walking in Central Park, Peter said to Jean, "Let's go to New Orleans and live our own life."

Jean actually was very reluctant to move away from her mother, father, brothers and sisters because she was very family oriented. But, being very much in love with Peter she said, "I'm going to miss my family, but wherever you go, I go." So off they went.

Dream

Why not dream————About the
Difference between now and then,
Between you and yourself,
Between beauty—and beauty lost.
A beautiful person dreams.
You are the handiwork of your dreams.
Go ahead—dream about love.
Be brave—dream about love.
Have faith————let love be your God,
Whatever anything means to you—
Yes you—nobody else.
Your life is *your* dream, even as it dances
With the dreams of others.
What a beautiful dance.
The mind is fond of its illusive reality.
It labels things like love
And dreams as unreal.
E=MC2 means reality of the mind
And *illusion only* is cast in stone.
But life is not.
Somewhere in between
Lies the truth about your dreams.
It's all so laughable.
Why not dream? It's all so loveable.
Why not dream?
You are that beautiful thing

That objectifies the mind.
Why not dream—
About so many wonderful things,
About not being caught
Between the truth and everything else.
So much to do, yet nothing to do.
There you are,
Being you and everything else,
With every one dancing the dance,
Watching the dance, being the dance.
What now my love?
It's only a dream—you are the life of it.
Be that—
Be anything you really want to be.
You know what it is.
Be honest.
It's the only thing that matters
When it becomes so beautiful
That it seems like a dream,
Believe and know that it's real.
It's why you are here.
Now is the time to live your dream—
In all its sweetness, in all its vitality,
In all its fatness, in all its charm.
In all its kindness and goodness,
In all its dynamics that take you
Where you really want to go.
It's your boat! Sail baby sail!

The wind is blowing your way.
You are at the helm,
The cool breeze and the sea spray
Are in your face.
Go, beautiful being, Go!
You are in full stream, full dream,
This is the real thing—
love has given you wings!
Love has made you strong!
You can do no wrong, it is who you are.
You thought it was a dream—
But it was the only real thing,
Even when it was only a ticket—
A piece of paper in your hand
To the greatest show on earth!
Your life and all it is meant to be—
Is in *that* dream—like Spring—
It is the one you *must* believe in!
Embrace it with all your heart.
The heart of hearts knows that dream
—And knows that experience.

7 New Orleans

One night at a club, they met some friends and Peter said to Jean, "Come on, we're going to smoke some tea." Jean didn't know what he was talking about, but it sounded kind of mysterious and fun, so without a word she left with them in their car and soon smelled a strange kind of smoke. Somebody passed her a hand-rolled cigarette and Peter said, "Inhale and hold it," in that funny tone everyone makes when they're trying to talk and hold their breath at the same time.

At first she couldn't detect anything, then suddenly she noticed that the moon was bigger and more beautiful than she had ever seen it, and her senses were suddenly more alive in a way she had never felt before. She wanted to touch the moon. There was also a subcultural connectedness she was experiencing with their new friends.

When they got back to the club there was live jazz and Jean said, "Let's dance!"

Peter replied, "Wait Jean, have a seat, this is listening music." Of course Jean thought, "How can you dance without listening to the music?"

but she sat and listened. Soon she was hearing
things she had never heard before. Dancing
is possible because the mind can actually do
numerous things at once. However, I think
when you learn to listen and dance without
thinking what you are doing next, dancing
becomes one with the music and the only focus
is the music itself. Listening instead of dancing
is an important step in getting to that point.
This is what Jean was discovering and this is
one thing she always loved about Peter. He was
always turning her on to new things. He shared
everything with her.

Peter was falling in love with Jazz, not that
he hadn't loved jazz for a long time, but now
he wanted to play the saxophone. "You know
what? All the good saxophone players are on the
West Coast." Maybe there's some truth to that,
in a temporary sort of way that seemed to be the
trend. So Jean, Peter and Mike were off to San
Francisco.

8 I Got My Start In San Francisco

Once they got there, the ocean had its magical way with him and he started dreaming once again about building boats and sailing. Of course, now that he had carpentry skills, he found a book by a famous boat builder with very sophisticated principles of design and methods and Peter decided he could build a boat. I've seen that book and I can only say it was not written for novices. However, Peter was brilliant at math and gifted with a conceptual mind that understood anything written or spoken. The next thing he had to do was to find a place to work. He found a place down by the piers where there was a junk yard and an old houseboat. It turned out the junk man needed a helper in exchange for use of the houseboat and a place to build a boat. Peter and the junk man became chums and Peter started building his first boat. My mom got a job at Schrafts on Market Street.

The San Francisco episode must have started in 1946 because I was born February 19, 1947 at Stanford Hospital. Jean worked as long as they would let her and Peter hauled junk and worked on the first of over one hundred boats he would build.

Building a boat was always exciting to watch. First Peter could be seen drawing the plans at night, then he would build the keel with laminations including allowance for the centerboard, if it was a shallow keel, which was the way he usually built boats for speed. A keel has much more drag and a centerboard can be adjusted for depth as needed (less depth more speed, but less control). Then he would build the ribs, sometimes with laminations, sometimes not. Then the sides and deck built around what would be the cabin, then mast, booms, rudder and he would have the sails made while doing painting and hardware. I was too young to know, but it must have been a very pretty sight seeing that first boat in the water. His boats always looked like a cross between a Viking ship replica and a New England lap-strake, pointed-stern fishing boat. And he always painted eyes on the bow. The sails were odd shaped rectangles and the curve from bow to stern was always very beautiful and graceful. I'm sure from the very beginning Krohn boats were unique works of artistic mobile sculpture. I've been told the maiden voyage across the San Francisco Bay to

Sausalito was both eventful and adventurous.
The winds and currents are very strong there
which is why they built a prison on the rock
island in the middle of the Bay. There was a lot
of upwind tacking, and being blown and dragged
off course, as well as near misses with the big
ships and cruisers going in and out of the Bay.
Sometime during the night they finally made it
across and the next day went through it all over
again. No Peugeot Sound that trip.

With the Krohns, big change was always on
the horizon. Peter had a fondness for stray dogs
and, of course, junk yards always need dogs.
One day Jean was home with baby Pat (me), and
toddler Mike, and the dogs and while she was in
the bathroom closing the window it came down
hard on her fingers which then became stuck. So
there she was for two hours with the boys crying
and the dogs barking in total misery until Ray
(the junk man) came by and freed her and took
her to the hospital. Her fingers were flattened
but not broken. Jean was unhappy. At the same
time she got a letter from her sister June back in
New York. She was getting married and wanted
Jean to be there.

9 Woodstock

Jean left first and Peter followed, after selling the boat. Peter heard that the artist Kuniyoshi was teaching art in Woodstock, New York, so that was the next residence for the Krohns. Actually Peter was still using his adopted father's name, so at this time we were the Wagners.

In 1948, Woodstock was a thriving art colony and their friends then were jazz musician Zoot Simms and Bob Kaufman (who would one day to be a Beat Poet), among other similar types. Somebody gave us a chicken coop to live in and soon Jean had it looking and feeling like a cabin in the woods. These were my earliest memories. Picking wild raspberries, rolling in the grass and getting itchy, water flies that looked like skaters when swimming and wading in the brook, the black rocks, a barn with horse tack and wasps, the earthy smell – and the green. I remember Bob Kaufman's bare feet for which he was famous, and flies catching on a fly strip. One day Grandma and Grandpa Pescia came and brought toys; a dump truck for Mike and a sand truck for me.

It was probably in Woodstock studying with Koniyoshi that Peter explored new ideas in artistic expression that reached more and more into the heart of the creative act as a state of being its own reality rather than an attempt at doing something which might be better done with a camera, yet not buying into that preconceived notion as being true, but simply opening up a new way of approaching art.

10 Florida

However, the itch of adventure and the approaching winter (which Peter wanted no part of) presented a new opportunity. Peter and Jean met someone from the Florida Keys that wanted to live in Woodstock. This man approached them saying, "I have a great boat building scene down in Marathon, let's switch scenes!" They took him up on it and were headed south.

Uncle Mike, Peter's brother, came up from NYC in his brand new copper-tan colored Buick convertible, with the air intake holes that made it look really hot, and took us to the Keys.

The new scene was a one-bedroom trailer parked behind a donut shop. We became friends with the donut maker who would give us boxes of glazed donuts, which we occasionally overindulged in, but Jean kept that activity in check. Having been trained as a nurse and brought up on a balanced diet, good nutrition was generally the rule, but those donuts were my first unforgettable eating experience!

We were soon back living on a boat and Peter went from boat building to crawfishing. One day, as I was sitting with my food in the cockpit of the boat and, having lost interest in what I was eating, I started to doze off. Before I knew it I was plummeting into the water, watching the green water all around me. I had no notion of swimming and no fear of drowning, but was simply allowing myself to be submerged in the experience of being under water. And that's the last thing I remember, but my mother who was doing dishes while I was floating under the water, happened to see me in the ocean and grabbed me by the hair and pulled me up on deck.

On August 4, 1949, my brother Lee was born and, a few months later, our family got on the front cover page of the *Saturday Evening Post* with a story inside with the heading "They wouldn't give up their home afloat for a mansion ashore." In the picture Jean is holding the infant Lee, I was almost three, Mike was five, and we're all sitting or standing around the boat cabin. Soon after, they sold the boat and we moved to New Orleans once again.

11 Trouble in New Orleans

Peter hungered for a chance to paint and New Orleans had a thriving art scene. In order to supplement his income from art, he started a picture framing business and was doing quite well until one night some very mean men in gray suits entered our house asking questions and giving orders in a rough tone of voice I had never known, but would later recognize in gangster movies.

"What's this?" one of them asked holding up a Kodak can big enough for a 35 mm role of film which I recognized as the container of this green cigarette making substance I had seen Peter roll and smoke, giving off a strange, heavy smelling fragrance I didn't care too much for.

Having no fear, I piped up, "That's my daddy's smoking tobacco!" letting them know they were walking on shaky ground. The Harrison act had just recently passed and they were trying to get convictions. They were there because of an informant trying to get off the hook by pointing the finger at someone else, and in this case, even accusing my father of dealing.

When Jean went to the jail to see Peter, he told her, "They're going to put me on a sugarcane plantation and beat me with a rubber hose for ten years!" Jean got her father to post the bail bond, and then we fled to Mexico.

12 South of the Border

Right or wrong, it seemed like the only thing
to do. We took the cheapest buses available;
the ones that went from village to village
transporting farmers and their livestock and
produce. I remember a lunatic lady that kept
hanging her coat on the buzzer cord designed
for stop requests. It drove the bus driver crazy.
This woman with dark hair and fair skin suffered
from a sort of other-worldliness, like she had
spent too much time gazing at the moon, and
seemed to be in a strange state of bliss where
everything was funny. It was impossible to get
mad at her.

We finally ended up in Mexico City where
Peter was able to use the G.I. Bill to get us
a huge apartment with two maids while he
attended art school at Mexico City College, as
well as studying with great Mexican painters like
Orosco and Diego Rivera.

Years later, I would realize the beauty of the
seeming time warp in Mexico City. Everything
was halfway between Victorian and Modern
(Art Deco style) or just old Mexican which is a
combination of old European and old 'whatever'

in bright colors, sometimes faded and/or chipped and flaky.

In many ways Mexico City is a romantic, poetic city of infinite magnitude. Pretty girls, handsome men, lovers pairing off all over the place, especially in parks and lots of intentional and unintentional sexual innuendo. At least that's my memory there in the 50's. Lots of boys and men of all ages riding bicycles with colorful tape and decorations and cyclists using a metal clip to keep their pants away from the greasy chain. The girls and women wore a vast array of colorful dresses. Boys like my big brother, Mike, and older ones played baseball in the park, or more likely, soccer, or as they call it "futbol" or played marbles or spun tops. Boys my age (4) mostly just wandered and watched the human drama of every day existence and the world that stages the playing out of it.

Refrigeration was still far from universal and I remember the ice man bringing a big block of ice for the "icebox", the precursor of the refrigerator. He carried it with one hand with the aid of big metal pinchers. He would release it with a kind of bowling motion and it would slide up to our door and he would yell "Yellow", which is Spanish for ice, but in Spanish is spelled hielo. At four I knew what color yellow was, but

I didn't know that in Spanish it was "amarillo" or that yellow in Spanish was the pronunciation for "ice." Those quizzical thought processes soon came to an end because children learn fast when they're dropped in the middle of a new national culture. Soon Peter and Jean were telling us, "Don't speak Spanish in the house because you'll forget your English." Most of the people in our lives, including the maids, spoke Spanish.

One of Peter and Jean's best friends at the time, however, was the writer Bill Burroughs, and I don't remember him ever-speaking Spanish. He was one of the few people with whom we could speak English, and it always gave me a warm feeling of familiarity that intrinsically created almost a family connection. He was very fatherly. I was always curious about the egg that was frequently leftover around his mouth even though it was way past breakfast. I guess when someone is high on heroin all the time, when that occurred, it was rather frivolous. Other than that he was a real New York gentleman: English without the accent, yet always correct in manner and speech; American English in a non-colloquial flavor, spoken smooth and cool, yet quite capable of expressing feeling, dressing and grooming conservatively but always interestingly and with a certain subtle flair, a kind masculinity with a twinkle in the eye, and a dry, clever wit.

That describes Bill Burroughs, Peter and maybe a handful of other men I have known. Reflections of the human experience as something other than you might see at the movies or on television, unless you were really lucky. In other words, the act of creating was a way of life. Unusual perceptions expressed as an act itself. Bill Burroughs was like a big brother to the artists, poets, musicians and the students of each, that were forming a cultural society on that particular edge of life, from people like Jack Kerouac, who was always trying to get my mother to shoplift, to Bill and Donna Hood, who had two boys the same age as Lee and me. Bill Hood was a fine musician perfecting his craft; a reed man who idolized Charlie Parker and would later become an important west coast musician, composer and arranger with people like Shorty Rogers, Bud Shank, Marty Paich, and Bill Holman.

At night Peter and Jean would go out to the Afro-Cuban clubs and dance. Afterwards they would bring home the musicians and play, sing and dance until the wee hours of the morning. Most of the time, we boys would sleep through it, but Jean said that one night I kept up a steady rhythm on a drum all night long. Meanwhile, Peter won first prize with a work of representational art, which he felt was important to master on the way to his own unique approach to art.

One day, Bill Burroughs told Peter and Jean that he had it on good word that the "Federales" were getting ready to come down hard on the bohemian community there and the best thing for us was to go to Yucatan.

We took a third-class bus to our first destination, Veracruz, a major port on the Gulf of Mexico, and at that time the only practical way to get from there to Yucatan was by boat. We spent the day on the beach between the water and the palapas—palm frond thatched shelters. The water, of course, was more fun, so we spent most of the day in the sun and this was the first time I remember getting sunburned. Late in the afternoon we boarded the boat to Yucatan. It was my first seasick experience. We landed in Campeche and got on a bus to a little town called Chichalu. We arrived late at night and found a friendly family that would let us share their palapa with them. I'm not sure if I slept at all that night because the dogs were barking and trying to frighten each other or us, or both, and there was no door on the entry to the palapa. I was almost certain the dogs would come inside and attack us. I was very relieved when the night ended and dawn arrived.

Almost everyone lived in palm frond thatched homes that were usually open to the breeze, and everybody slept, were born, and made love in hammocks. The women cooked over fires on wood-burning stoves made of bricks. The women wore white dresses that were draped loosely over their bodies, instead of form fitting, and had short or no sleeves. The hem and neck openings, which were broad almost to the shoulder, were ornately decorated with large brightly colored embroidered flowers. The men dressed in khaki. Everyone wore light shoes or sandals or boots. A lot of people went barefoot.

I'm sure Peter was at a loss for exactly what to do. Most of the people in Chichalu were fisherman and farmers. This was an interesting juncture in Peter's life as a young man. Up to now he had been creating his identity as an artist, a boat builder, a sculptor, a craftsman. This seemed a meditative, reflective time. Peter spent many hours contemplating the nature of life and observing these primitive people and the natural beauty that ran through their lives like a golden cord. He had studied art, design, naval architecture and furniture, developing his objective abilities that were complemented by his subjective sense that moved him from the inside. But this was a time when he found himself in a nonintellectual world of people happily experiencing life simply, sensually and intuitively. Jean, on the other hand, was automatically drawn in to this new primitive culture and allowed herself to be a part of doing all the things the Mayan women did because they invited her to participate in their morning to sundown activities. The people adopted us; Jean learned how to make tortillas and helped the women. My brother Mike, seven years old at the time, got a job making the rounds at 4:00 a.m. with the baker, and I got to go with them once. The baker put his big round tin (about three or four feet in diameter and six inches deep) full of pan dulce (Mexican pastry), which he sold to the fisherman before they went out. Eventually I got a job selling peanuts. I would wait for the bus to come from Progresso and the driver would have a large bag of peanuts (supermarket size), which I would take to the baker who would roast them for me. I then took them home and wrapped them with newspaper into small four-ounce packages, then put them into a burlap sack and went to the outdoor movie theater. Before the movie started and during intermission, I would walk up and down the aisle calling out "cacahuates, cacahuates (cah-cah-wah-tays) de veinte (vain-tay) centavos!" which in English would be, "Peanuts, Peanuts for twenty cents!?

We were all becoming one with the spirit and ways of these beautiful Mayan people. On further reflection, I am very moved realizing that there we were, a destitute American family from a completely different culture, being saved by the most humble and lovely kind of people who absorbed us readily, cheerfully and enthusiastically into their lives. Besides worship, I remember two things they did as a community. When the minnow called "sac" (sock) would be running, all the men would take long nets shaped like tennis nets and in waist-deep water would herd them onto the beach and into the nets by the thousands and dry them in the sun on concrete slabs about 20 feet by 50 feet—a bounty they would share and which would last quite a while. They would also share boats. I remember them bringing in a whale shark that filled a whole boat – 18 feet, stem to stern and 5 to 6 feet wide.

Another thing they did was dance in the main square on Saturday nights. Everybody danced – young, old and in between. We would spend our days walking around, visiting people, eating sea grapes (a grape that grows on small trees and with leaves that look like grape leaves except they're much harder and thicker), that hung in clusters but had large seeds like cherry pits, and cactus pears and mangos.

At one point we lived outside town a ways at a resort called *Cocoteros* or Coconut Grove. Jean worked as a waitress and Peter did carpentry work. I remember one time Peter walked into our room and a very large scorpion landed on his shoulder. Peter batted it off without further consequence but once again we were reminded of the danger lurking in the shadows in this primitive land. Another time, Peter and Jean were walking home late at night when they became aware of a mysterious dark figure following them, popping in and out of the dark shadows. When he came close they turned around and saw a man draped in a black cape that was drawn across his face with his hand and forearm and only his eyes visible. He stood like that and stared at them and then showed his pointy, canine looking teeth. Then he turned around and disappeared into the shadows. But the days were bright and wild and natural.

In time, Peter got a job at a lumber mill teaching them how to make plywood, a technology not yet introduced in Yucatan. After that, the mill owner wanted to start a boat building business. So Peter started building a boat on the beach in a little town near Progresso called Seiba Playa. When the boat was finished, we went on sailing trips and started living on the boat.

On one of my wanderings, I saw a boy in the park playing with some puppies. After playing with the puppies for a while he asked me if I wanted one. I said "Sure!" I imagine Peter and Jean were somewhat shocked, but they nevertheless relented and Peter named her Fawn because she looked like a baby deer.

One day, Peter said, "When we go back to the States we'll take my father Russell Krohn's name. Instead of being the Wagners, we'll be the Krohns." So, we became the Krohns, and sailed the various coves and beaches, living off what we caught – usually snappers, grunts, angelfish and so forth.

One night while sailing under the moon and stars we hit something and began to take on water. The next thing we knew everything was under water except part of the deck and the cabin. The moon had gone down and there we were, two miles out, sitting on top of the cabin; mom, dad, three boys and Fawn, in a pitch-dark night. I forget how long we sat there like that, but eventually some lights appeared in the distance. Peter was yelling "S.O.S.!" He was very loud, but not loud enough so he told us all to start yelling. We had no lights due to water immersion, but we must have been loud enough because they eventually came close to shine their spotlight on us and pull us up onto their shrimp boat. It must have been a very large boat because they were able to get our boat (which by the way was named the Gaviota, that in Spanish means the Seagull) up on the deck of the shrimp boat.

It was a three-man crew. Ryan was the skipper, a fatherly family man with an aura of someone who knew how to accept and deal with responsibility, a man who always had a ready smile, good advice, and made you feel like you were an important person in his life, just because you had become his friend. I only remember one of the other two, and his name was Andy, a guy who was always the life of any party, always joking and saying things like, "Wait till you see this!" or, "Let's do that!" and, "Isn't that something!"

Eventually, years later, we progressed to become vegetarians, but at this time we were omnivores and ate whatever was available. Popular foods among the Mayans were shark, deer, armadillo, pork, beef, cabbage, squash, mangos, oranges, watermelons, fish, beans and corn. Jean used to amaze and amuse the fisherman because she had a standing order for octopus, which they didn't eat and therefore was free. She also had a cookbook from our previous life, which I always enjoyed perusing because of the pictures of cake, ham and other gorgeous dishes, the savoring of which were just beyond my imagination.

In the hold of the shrimp boat was a case of Foster's Frosty Root Beer which I'm pretty sure is a thing of the past now, and a box of sweet, juicy, crispy, red delicious apples which were treats from another world. Ryan and the crew were from St. Petersburg, Florida, and were there for the shrimp and to salvage a boat – the very one that punched a hole in the bottom of ours – that had been lost recently in the vicinity by a friend.

The next day we were paid a visit by the Mexican Coast guard. First of all, they were angry about the Americans fishing in their waters, and secondly, about what they considered stealing of Mexican property, because they had the sole right to salvage anything in their waters. At any rate, they let us go but the shrimp boat retrieval was out of the question.

Incredibly enough, after leaving our repaired sailboat anchored in a lagoon, we went shrimping with our new friends for a few days,. When we returned for the boat it was gone. (Thirty years later, Peter was dining at a Mexican restaurant in California and after telling the boat story, a Mexican from the next table over said he lived in a Yucatan village near Progresso and that they had taken possession of the boat thinking it had been abandoned. He said they had been using that boat to feed the village for many years.)

"That was the boat we were going to sail back to Florida in," Peter told Ryan.

"We'll take you back to Seiba Playa, Ryan answered, and when we get things settled with the Mexican Government we'll take you back to the States with us," which was of course better than sailing to Florida in a small sailboat with no motor.

So our time in Mexico was coming to an end. After two years living with the Mayans, we had become part of their lives and they were our people. "Tu no puedes ir a los Estados Unidos, tu eres Mexicano." Although I was thoroughly bi-cultural and can't remember when I was thinking in Spanish or English, what they were telling me was I couldn't go back because I was Mexican now. Truly, I did feel more Mexican than American, but I knew that was coming to a close.

Too young to be sentimental, I suppose, I was nevertheless leaving a life rich in soul and spirit and love from people that were as pure, simple and unquestioning as life itself. Life does not ask questions, it just lives. In our minds we ask questions because of need. We also have a need to feel free from questions and just live and experience life. The only really important question is ultimately how to best ride this wave of life that we have been given. Once you are born you are on it, and need to be with it as it goes on, not stopping for your questions. Suddenly, the mind does something miraculous. In the middle of all this conscious and subconscious connecting, analyzing and conceptualizing, it creates a space that feels like we can stop there and think, and we really can't because the mind is in a never-ending slavery to thought. Time, because of its ephemeral nature, is an illusion. It just keeps coming and going from nowhere to nowhere. Take away the illusion and what do you have? Nothing. Yet there you are. The real thing is you.

I Gave No Thought

When I was born,
When Love, took earthly form,
When Life, amazed me so,
When I fell into the sea,
When I bounced gently on the bottom,

I gave no thought.
When I looked up at the sun and stared,
When I saw the beauty of nature,
When the dancing began,
When we laughed,
When we played,
I gave no thought.
When sailing at sea,
When the wind and water
Sprayed my face,
As I wandered about,
When I started to think,
I gave no thought.

There I was, seven years old, and I knew
this without knowing I knew. The neat thing
about being a kid is you're really just along for
the ride, hoping to learn the ropes, hoping to
have learning experiences intense and powerful
enough to leave marks that will last. Indelible
marks. As I write, I am looking at a mark, a scar
on my left index knuckle. Still there after more
than fifty years, reminding me of the power of
a sharp knife and a people that knew how to
live the life they were given, which itself was
an unspoken love deeply woven into a fabric of
laughter, tears, music, work, family and friends.

Life can be perceived as a series of dilemmas, and each one is the dilemma of a lifetime. You can get perfect waves that you just get on and ride, a perfect curl or shoulder with a break so seamless that it is more of a perfect vortex of water in motion than a break. However, most waves break unevenly, which I think makes them more interesting. There are waves in Laguna Beach between St. Ann and Thalia Street that start off with an impossible break that 'closes out' (making it impossible to stay ahead of the break) if you start to ride it straight in, but if you can turn left it becomes a ridable wave. Life is like that. You see a dilemma coming that could wipe you out and you maneuver your way out of it. Sometimes it seems like destiny makes a maneuver for you. Such was our case when we left Yucatan in 1953. I suppose we could have lived there forever, but it was time for a change. A dilemma's resolution almost always means change.

13 Adios to Mexico
Going Home to the US of A

Next thing you know, I was standing on the bow of a large shrimp boat, watching the porpoises and flying fish jump and fly ahead of the wake caused by the boat. We were crossing or cruising the Gulf Stream, which was full of fish of all kinds.

"Tell Pat about the time I pulled a flying fish out of the air" exclaimed Andy, in a sincere yet joking voice. There were sharks of all kinds. The big ones had pilot fish that glued themselves onto the sharks' backs by suction devices implanted by nature, especially the really big whale sharks that just kind of floated on top of the water. Every once in a while a huge Manta Ray with a wingspan of five to 10 feet would fly up out of the water and fall back down with a big splash. These kinds of adventures and the root beer and apples in the hold kept us busy for the three days it took to cross the Gulf of Mexico at about 8 knots.

Early morning on the third day there were black specks on the horizon. Land! Land! Land!

Jean was baking blueberry tarts, and we were eating them as the Sunshine Skyway across the Tampa Bay came into sight. It was our introduction into the modern world. A ten-mile long bridge hundreds of feet high at the center with a large spanning structure that reached up into the sky sparkled and beamed in the Florida sun.

When we pulled into the wharf in Tampa there were men in uniform asking questions. Once the necessary lies were told, we were on our way to St. Petersburg to stay with Ryan and his family until we could get our own place. The modern infrastructure was so different from the life we were used to. Lee was still asking for "agua" when he wanted water. From a primitive world of sand and water, and a lifestyle mostly fashioned from the jungle, we were plunging into a world of street life with cars and homes with trees, lawns, and sidewalks. Inside the houses were refrigerators, gas stoves, carpets, couches, ottomans and television! (Television never became part of *our* home.) Garbage trucks! What an awesome piece of machinery that was! Construction workers had yellow heavy-duty machinery like backhoes with big steel scoops on the front. A very different world this was.

14 Life in Florida

Peter got a job at a boat building business in Sarasota. We moved into the upstairs of a two-story wooden duplex, with a nice lady downstairs and across the way that always offered us apple butter sandwiches. My first friend was a boy my age down the street named Mack. His father was an airline pilot who had flown bombers in World War II. We played with his toy planes and cars and climbed trees.

It was May of 1954, and I was just starting first grade. It's amazing how I just fell right into it. For the first time in my life, I was part of a group of my peers. A child's cup is always pretty much empty, always quite ready for new knowledge and experiences. By the time you get to be seven years old, you have assimilated volumes of life's knowledge and experiences, yet everything is new. Peter and Jean were very liberal about our comings and goings. Once we had breakfast, the only responsibility was to be home for dinner. The world was ours to explore and make friends with. At night, we liked Jean to read to us.

Even though I didn't fully understand, my father was a fugitive, and we were now the

Krohns, avoiding things like drivers licenses and phone numbers for the next ten years. Peter and Jean's caution reinforced their detached view of society and supported the truths that Peter and Jean were recognizing about life. In their excitement and pleasure to be back in their true home country, they were still able to see through the transparent values of materialism, and the lack of real truth in the lives of most people being brainwashed by television and other media that defined modern American life. After all, Peter was still a real artist that would never sell his talents for commercial purposes and still painted eyes on his boats, and they danced at the drop of a hat, and Jean was a writer and poet. They were still the same nonconformist idealists that started shaping their ideals with Kuniyoshi and Zoot Sims in Woodstock, Mexico City, New York City, New Orleans, and San Francisco with their bohemian friends like Bob Kaufman, George Connely, Jack Kerouac and Bill Burroughs. The difference was that they now had the experience of living a very primitive life with the Mayans for two years.

It was a full decade before the hippy revolution when everybody talked about love. Love was so intrinsic to the fabric of our life that it was never mentioned. It seems love gets talked about if it's missing, and then it always sounds like a sermon. When you try to put it into words it becomes less that what it really is. Love is its own expression. We know it when we feel it, hear it, are touched by it, smell its fragrance, move by its rhythm and melody, when it frees our mind, when it reverberates through our being, when we simply have to give it, and we do because we've tasted its sweetness and know that's what it's meant for. To the intellectual it may seem intangible but, in truth, all else is intangible. The artist, the poet, the musician achieve their goal when they create an experience that allows the appreciator to catch that experience as a real part of life, hence this poem by Jean Krohn (now Jean Lindsay).

Lovers

> The artist is between the sight
> And the feeling,
> The musician is between the sound
> and the feeling,
> The poet is between the word
> And the feeling,
> L o v e r s are the Feeling.

But Peter was a fugitive. He had given four of the best years of his life in defense of our country. His sanity had been pushed to limits we can only imagine. He was proud of his part in vanquishing the Nazi Empire and their evil allies. But now the price he had to pay for his freedom was to disconnect himself and his family from family ties, telephone service, driving privileges. We were the "rolling Krohns." We were a living demonstration of the "rolling stone gathers no moss" metaphor. Like a Charlie Parker solo, our life was improvisational.

Ever since the early New York City artist years, Peter had always associated himself with a local Art Students League, be it in New York City, Woodstock, New Orleans, Mexico City, Sarasota or others. There, Peter and Jean always found kindred bohemian souls.

In Sarasota, Peter had gotten a job as art director for the annual float that Ringling Brothers and Barnum and Bailey Circus would enter into the Sarasota Pageant. Every spring this local parade commemorated the Spanish Colonial days. Meanwhile, he made friends with a very enjoyable couple; Eric Von Schmidt and his girlfriend, Bonnie. Eric was an artist and folk musician who knew lots of songs and was a very talented singer, guitar player and generally upbeat presence. We were now by the bayou and there was plenty of room for a boat to be built, so Peter was building a wooden sailboat and Eric was building one just like it right next to Peter's. It was Eric's first boat and he was following Peter step by step.

Peter and Jean had made friends with a photographer and his wife, Tooni and Ralph Coolidge, who eventually became our best friends. The Coolidges lived in an upstairs studio overlooking the main street, leading up to the center of town called "Five Points." It was the street coming up from the pier on Sarasota Bay. From their windows we had the best seats in town when the Parade went by with the High School marching band and floats. The Circus float was quite spectacular, the centerpiece being a large elfish clown, its attire painted in many colors and designs. Another highlight was the marching band of the Negro High School. They dressed in bright white, blue and silver, and played a variety of exciting rhythms, and their marching was more like dancing.

Soon, it was summer and Peter and Jean's boat the "Sandpiper" was finished. Eric's soon would be, and he stayed on and moved into the Bayou house to finish his boat. We launched our boat, which was our new home, into the bayou and followed it out to the Sarasota Bay. We hoisted the sails, which were a mizzen, mainsail, and a jib, quite a lot of sail for a 26 foot boat, which had a center board eliminating drag for maximum sailing speed.

We headed for the Tampa Bay. She handled very nicely and was fast. Soon it was night and we were gliding across the Tampa Bay under a full moon that reflected on the gently rippling surface of the water – moonlight dancing to the melodious and rhythmic sound of the Sandpiper peacefully plying its way through the water, gently sailing along after a warm summer breeze which seemed to caress the sails as it filled them with its gentle power, just going, going and going, not caring if we ever got there. We could see the porpoises in the moonlight, undulating, propelling themselves along side from time to time, going up and down like a dance and occasionally blowing water out of the holes in the top of their heads. Porpoises are like dolphins, so instead of a dolphin dance, this was a porpoise dance. The great Persian Poet, Hafiz, wrote almost 700 years ago in his poem:

Where Dolphins Dance

I have become very Consciousness
Upon whom we all play.
Thus my eyes have filled with warm,
Soft oceans of Divine Music
Where jeweled dolphins dance
Then leap into this world.**

Seeing such creatures cavort in the wild is such
a pleasure. It was a special moment for Peter
and me, while everyone else was down below
sleeping, and he told me about the channel
markers, and geographical points that related
to the charts, and different kinds of winds and
breezes, the sails and movement of the boat –
and what a lovely creature she was. Soon I was
falling asleep and went down below to find a
place for sleep.

In the morning, I was usually the first one
up. I walked up to the bow and peed into the
quiet waters where Peter had anchored us, off
one of the many Keys that dot the Gulf Coast
of Florida. I sat in the cockpit and watched the
birds that were already up getting their breakfast.

---

* "The Subject Tonight is Love – 60 Wild and Sweet Poems of
  Hafiz"—Versions by Daniel Ladinsky

Soon, Jean was fixing oatmeal. When breakfast was finished, the sails would be hoisted and away we went with the first breeze. Soon we were out in the Gulf where the wind was better and so it went, with the porpoises cavorting around us during the day and scratching their backs on the barnacled bottom of the boat at night as our constant companions.

When we came upon a river, we would go inland on it until we desired to go back to the open sea. Up one river we discovered a Greek fishing village called Tarpon Springs. A lot of the rivers in Florida are fed by springs. Here the Greeks fished for sponges in the Gulf, a dangerous occupation that requires them to go down in extremely heavy suits that allow them to breathe and walk on the bottom of the sea where the sponges grow. All the equipment has to work perfectly in the face of natural forces or the diver risks losing his life support. The Greek boats are quite interesting with the sweeping curve of the top of the hull from bow stem to stern and the placement of the cabin at the stern. With their Zorba-esque personalities, the fishermen were a lot of fun. On one river an eight-foot shark came close to the surface sideways, as if to get a good look at us. He had probably been feasting in the brackish waters and was curious as to the nature of his gigantic competition. Needless to say, we didn't swim in that river.

One of my favorites was Crystal river, which had a gigantic spring situated in a lagoon with a sandy bottom that reflected the blue sky through the clear fresh water. The water came gushing out of a large hole that I would try to swim into but the force was too strong. That kind of constant water flow is a wonder of nature to me. The name of the town was Yankee Town, which was strange because that part of Florida was mostly small town southern folk that would incorporate the term "ya'll" in their speech constantly with the most sweet southern accent. "Where ya'll from? Ya'll like to go to the movie? Ya'll fish?" It actually turns out to be a verbally economical way to talk.

Everywhere we went, people were fascinated by our family of five who would just come sailing into their lives. By the time we got to Cedar Keys we were broke, but Peter was able to earn some money fixing crab traps. On our way back to the Tampa Bay area, a swimmer in Clearwater (which was a small beach town in those days) swam out to our boat out of curiosity, struck up a friendship and asked us to his house for dinner. He lived on the beach, so we anchored and had dinner with him and his family. The next morning we were on our way to St. Petersburg with some army C-rations he had given us.

There was one terrifying event I forgot to mention on our trip north. We were about a half-mile out at the mouth of a river when we saw two tornadoes about a half-mile inland (east) and a half-mile south of us. They looked like the waterspouts you sometimes see way out on the water in Florida, except these were on land headed for the water towards us. The wind was blowing so hard, Peter reefed the sails with our help and then told us all to go down below and pray (Peter was an atheist). We were doing about 20 knots (very fast) when we hit an oyster bar. I thought the bottom of the boat would tear open. The crushing noise was very loud and ferocious as we tried to sail away from the tornadoes that had turned into waterspouts. Jean was Catholic so we were saying a lot of Hail Marys and Our Fathers. The violent weather was probably over in less than an hour but it seemed to go on for hours. When something like that is over and you are still alive, life seems so sweet and beautiful. Fiber-glassing the bottom of the boat was a fairly new technique in 1955. I don't remember any other boats done like that back then. Everything had to be state-of-the-art good for Peter and it probably saved our lives. In fact, the Sandpiper had a double layer of Fiberglass on the bottom and eighteen inches up the sides.

St. Petersburg had a little marina right off the Tampa Bay just south of the municipal pier. To our astonishment, the street running by the marina and up to the pier was lined with mango trees: we would not go hungry. Nobody else seemed to eat them. In fact an old man said, "You'd better not eat those oranges, they're poison." We just laughed and never got sick. One day we went for a sail and saw another sailboat going the same way we were. We were tacking (maneuvering upwind) and basically sailing circles around them, but it was all in fun as theirs was not a particularly fast boat, while ours was. They were enjoying watching our unique craft sail and told us to meet them in Madeira Beach. We pulled up to their dock and got acquainted. Roy, the tall one, owned and ran the Snug Harbor Marina where we were docked, and Kirk owned the boat we were racing against. They said they wanted to buy our boat and Peter could build boats there. So Peter started building boats, each one different from the others, beautiful and interesting. There was a boat called the "Melody" docked there, which we lived on.

When we boys weren't going to school, we were fishing, swimming, playing baseball, or just wandering around this fascinating world of boats, fishermen, retirees and tourists. Jean took care of meals and helped Peter. Everybody wanted to talk about boats with Peter or take knot-tying lessons. Years before, Peter made it his business to learn how to tie all the knots relating to boats. As a boat builder and seaman, it was important to be knowledgeable in all aspects that he would be expected to know. One day a tall energetic guy named Dean Arnold came to talk about boats. Peter designed and helped build a large 38-foot boat for Dean. This one had a large flat transom. Dean had a $500 a month allowance (which was a lot of money in '55-'56) plus access to more because his Aunt was a major owner of 7-Up. The boat was called the Antigua. Dean really loved his boat. He and his girlfriend Jo moved into it and were very content for a while.

After about a year, we moved to an abandoned fish house (a dwelling designed as a place for fishing boats to bring in their fish, store them on ice and transfer them to land transportation) where there was room enough at the Marina to build a Catamaran. Instead of a regular mast, this one had an A-frame mast. Dean and Jo

moved into a house across from the fish house.
Soon the Catamaran was finished. We were
supposed to meet at a mooring sight after school.
It took longer than anticipated to get there, and
I saw them out there sailing around. I yelled but
they were too far away to hear so I went back to
the fish house feeling all alone for the first time
in my life.

I Cry

I am so far from home,
Far from my home.
There they go,
On the way to adventure,
On the way home, the one boy alone
In the wilderness makes me cry,
Sweet sadness is the sound
Of my heart,
My fragile consciousness
Awaits the mighty hand of God
In all its gentleness.
Just to be with you my dear
To touch the glowing tenderness
That makes me cry,
Why is it thus? Why do I ask?
How will the answer come?
The waves come crashing down

Against the rocks
With thundering soul
Against this lost world
And the boy cries out
And a hand comes out
To put him on the shore
Of that lost world,
Crying in the mist,
The mist that is everywhere,
Mostly unseen because
The illusion seems so real,
Like the hunger that can never be filled
By what's around.
Yet there is a beauty and kindness
In this cry, I cry for love!
I cry for the loneliness
In a different kind of mist
Full of magic, wonder
And poetry unspoken, music unplayed,
The human expression about to be,
Feeling the presence of God,
Like a friend who cares.
It must be love,
Nothing else is like it.
Nothing else makes me cry,
And the tears really are like
Very exquisite, unusual pearls
The very absolute

Epitome of preciousness.
Maybe we are here to cry like this.

We sailed to Sarasota. During that trip the
rudder broke and adjustments had to be made
to keep us from sailing backwards when she was
tacking against the wind. Sailing backwards is a
weird sensation.

In Sarasota we made friends with a Jewish
couple, Elihu, Joan, and their daughter, Kaya.
They were an interesting, artistic and intellectual
couple. She was a nurse and he was a writer.
Their home was artistically modern, but small,
and they let us live there while they were gone.
When they got back, we moved into a large shed
in the back. Dean came and visited frequently
which was always a lot of fun. Peter was now
back into painting and was showing in Sarasota
and around the Tampa Bay area. I was into Elvis
Presley. At school the girls would beg me to sing
"Blue Suede Shoes" or "Hound Dog" or "Don't
be Cruel." When I did they would chase me
around the school like the rabid Presley fans they
were. Of course, it didn't hurt that I had a mop
of hair and Presley wave.

Dean talked Peter and Jean into building a
camper on the back of Dean's forties pickup
and taking a trip to Mexico City. Peter, Jean and

Dean sat up in the cab and we three boys rode
in the back. We spent the whole trip looking out
the back which was kind of fun. Your immediate
view is up close and then you watch it get
smaller. In the front looking forward, the distant
view gets bigger and the up-close disappears
instantly. The surprise of the up-close in the back
is fun, but in the front you can see something
in the distance and then you're prepared for that
split second when it's up close. Either way, its
fleeting. Moments do not wait, they come and
they go, but sometimes you would like to hold
them there, to savor, to see, feel, touch, or hear,
or smell a little; so many things happen at once
you know there was something about it you
missed.

This was back in 1957 and there was no
freeway on this trip. We drove through each
little town and big city. We saw people where
they stood, walked or sat, where they talked,
played, ran, worked, looked, pointed, posed,
skipped, danced, snoozed, laughed, hollered,
and all the other things people do. So many
beautiful souls caught up in a drama, comedy
or circumstances we call daily life. We saw green
pastures, woods, red dirt, yellow dirt, black dirt,
brown dirt, sandy beaches along rivers and the
Gulf. We crossed the Mighty Muddy Mississippi

and it seemed to be a mile wide. We saw tidy neighborhoods with flowers, slums with flowers, laundry hanging out, many versions of Main Street, USA, horses, cows, sheep and dogs, the bayou country, and finally Texas along the Gulf. Then we went down into Mexico.

15 Mexico – Part 2

It seemed like so much time had passed. So much life had been lived. Mexico seemed to have a completely new flavor to me. Mike still remembered his Spanish but Lee and I had forgotten it. The homes, cars, and the businesses were from a completely different era of living from what we had now become accustomed to in the U.S. However, the cultural difference was enjoyable. The people were very friendly. The economic lifestyles were so varied. School children usually had uniforms. In the nice neighborhoods the gates, barred windows and walls with broken glass embedded on top, were evidence that if you were well off, you needed to secure your lifestyle. But it was just part of life. The rich, poor and in between shared daily life together, seemingly quite comfortably. Life was old with a different kind of newness here, and was intrinsically pretty. The feeling of soul was out in the open. There were many curious people, with a hundred questions about what we were doing there in that old Ford pickup. I think that was how we started remembering our Spanish.

As we got further south the land was more lush and green and the people more colorful, but the economic and social strata were the same. The poorest people were the most fun. The poor were not homeless but their abodes were more humble. Fifty plus years later it's still like that.

It was late at night when we were climbing the mountains to Mexico City. The next morning we were driving around Mexico City and the first place we stopped was a Dairy Queen. Dean was already getting homesick, while for us this felt like coming home. In those days there was the Dairy Queen, Sears and Sanborns, but everything else was pure Mexico. We finally found a hotel in the Roma Colony, or "La Colonia Roma" in Spanish. The districts were called colonies. The name of the hotel was "El Campo de Amor." I guess it was meant to be a place where lovers came. At any rate, it was inexpensive and clean. Dean didn't last very long. He couldn't speak the language and wanted to go back to Florida. Before the week was out he was gone.

Eating was very inexpensive. It was 12.5 pesos to the dollar. You could buy "La Comida Corrida" for five pesos (forty cents American then). That was the main meal of the day, usually eaten around 2 p.m. It was seven courses consisting of soup, salad, beans, rice, entree, tortillas and dessert. For breakfast we could buy enough pan dulce (Mexican pastry) for three pesos for the whole family. The three of us boys used to enjoy traveling around the city on buses. You could go just about anywhere for 20 centavos (1 and one half cents American), and if it was really far it was 50 centavos. We used to go to Chapultepec Park and buy soft, hot potato and cilantro tacos for ten centavos and wash them down with lemonade for another 10 centavos from a jovial elderly Indian lady. Chapultepec was like Central Park in New York City except it was a bright tropical green. Sometimes we'd get into a soccer or baseball game. Right near the hotel was a movie theater with an admission of one peso and fifty centavos. It was mostly Hollywood movies with Spanish subtitles, but some of the movies were Mexican, which were also interesting and enjoyable. That was where we saw "Angels with Dirty Faces," with James Cagney and Humphrey Bogart. This made an indelible impression with Mike. After that, he always wanted to be a bad guy with a good heart.

Before long, we moved into an apartment. There was evidently no hot water because whatever heated up the shower had to be fed by compressed wood-chip logs. Peter and Jean got jobs teaching English at the University of Mexico. We spent most of our days playing and enjoying good times with friends we made in the neighborhood. The local boys liked to paint little plastic cars with model enamel so they looked custom, and then we would draw curvy chalk race courses and push the cars with one push as far as it would go before it went off course, taking turns on our way to the finish line. Then there was volleyball, hopscotch and marbles, a kind of baseball played with a rubber ball and your fist instead of a bat.

Eventually, we would go inside, put on records and dance. There was a sort of pre-adolescent romance that I am still fond of remembering. The girls were fun and great dance teachers, teaching us swing dancing to Glenn Miller, and the cha cha and mambo to tropical music. We, in turn, taught them how to rock and roll to Elvis. All sweet memories. There was an indefinable sweetness in those friendships.

Then one night everyone's world changed. We awoke in the middle of the night to the building swaying and sirens wailing all over the city. There was a feeling of the ground rolling under the building. Pipes were breaking and walls cracking. Soon it all stopped, but the sirens kept going all night long. It was the earthquake of 1957 and it killed over 1,000 people. There were gaping cracks where roads had split open, buildings turned into a pile of rubble with people inside, buildings that fell into streets, buildings that hung in undulating arches over roads. Everyone had building damage. In the following week, the Hong Kong Flu of 1957 hit and everybody got it, or so it seemed.

When things recovered and settled down, we all took a trip to Acapulco to join up with our friend Feliz and the other Afro-Cuban musicians who played in his band.

16 Back to Stateside

Peter and Jean's jobs teaching English at the University of Mexico had come to an end. The winds of change were blowing back to the States. Dean Arnold told Peter, "I was responsible for getting you down there, so I'm responsible for getting you back," and soon we were flying back to Florida.

Dean was such a cool guy. He went down to Miami to pick us up and brought us back to Madeira Beach, where Peter was needed to do some boat work. Meanwhile, there was an opening at the Ringling Art Museum in Sarasota and Peter got the job. He was required to restore the very large picture frames on the massive Rubens and Rembrandt paintings which were 12 foot by 12 foot or larger. The Ringling had the largest Baroque art collection in the U.S. Peter's plan was to build a boat during the day and work at the Museum at night, and somehow find time to paint.

We moved into an army barracks near the Museum, on the outskirts of town, by the airport. There was a very cute hillbilly girl with brown-blond hair that I became infatuated with, but I was shy and preoccupied with baseball, bikes and more important things, so nothing happened there for a while.

One night just after sunset, Teresa was standing outside her house and she said "Hi Pat, let's listen to some Hillbilly music. We can sit in my uncle's car." How intriguing that seemed to me. Sitting in her uncle's car, I was both charmed and fascinated. She had the keys and was able to turn on the radio. We sat in the plush, chrome-accented interior listening to sweet strains of romantic hillbilly music (they now call it country and western.) It was one of my fondest memories of childhood.

Our evenings were spent reading, listening to records and dancing. On Fridays Jean would bake a cake, usually chocolate, and we would go to the Oslo Theater and see foreign films. The Oslo Theater was part of the Ringling Art Museum so we got in for free. We saw movies like Akiro Kurosawa's "Rashoman" and other movies by the major French, Italian and German producers of the day. The King of Norway had built the Oslo Theater during the Baroque period, and while probably no taller than a three-story building, it actually had five balcony levels built around the floor seating, like a horseshoe. The balcony levels were divided into booths large enough for 4 to 6 people. It was all wood with lots of ornate trimmings. John Ringling had it shipped to Sarasota during the boom years before the great depression, piece by piece like a jigsaw puzzle, and it was reassembled behind the museum. One time we saw a Danish opera there.

I wasn't able to get to Little League practice as regularly as desired and, as a result, I didn't get a lot of play time, and we lost all but one of our games. I remember I hit doubles on two occasions and struck out twice. I had gotten used to fast pitching and loved to hit. Sports were one of those things where I seemed to vacillate between mediocrity and stardom. Really strange things seemed to happen to me. One day when playing playground softball, I was playing shortstop and they kept hitting the ball at me. Inning after inning – grounders, bloops, pop-ups, and line drives – batter after batter, inning after inning, the ball kept coming to me – no hits, no runs, no errors. This went on for five innings.

My fifth grade teacher, Mrs. Tacket, was the kind of teacher everybody loved. She made hard things like long division seem easy. Her class was interesting: science, geography, social studies, the three R's and music. She played violin in the

Sarasota Symphony orchestra, taught us about the instruments and took us to a performance of Peter and the Wolf.

The summer of '58 was spent biking, playing ball, going to the beach, singing and dancing. We had a great Louis Armstrong record and we liked to dance to "When the Saints Go Marching In." One time a bunch of kids in the barracks got together and we performed with and for each other, ending it by parading around the barracks in a conga line singing, "When the Saints Go Marching In."

Since my big brother Mike was so charismatic and there was never enough of him to go around, I guess they asked if he had a brother, so he invited me to come along with him to the Friday Night dance at the Youth Center. "You'll have to tell anybody that asks that you're twelve" was the word. I became a regular because I loved to dance and I liked older girls. My girlfriends became the ones who liked dancing with me the most. Betty was my first girlfriend. We danced a lot and then she asked me to go on her church's hayride with her. I say 'girlfriend' because I was discovering the romantic element that seemed to resonate with a particular girl. We were the only ones on the hayride with a romantic connection, and I wanted to kiss her, but not as a sideshow for everybody else. It was fun anyway. She soon found someone her own age.

Then there was the tall brown-haired Jean Williams. We met at the movies after dancing the night before. We saw "The Blob." She was a ninth grader and had an ex-boyfriend or wannabe boyfriend who was a high school football player. Needless to say, it was very intimidating when he sat behind us making fun. She invited me to visit her at home, which I did one very lovely afternoon. Jean was into horses. I was not yet twelve and she was fifteen with beautiful lips and breasts. We had this romantic relationship, yet we never kissed. It was just the fringe benefits of the whole dancing thing, and I wasn't ready to make moves.

Peter and Jean were the dynamic duo; Peter painting and having shows, restoring gigantic frames at the museum, and building the boat during the day, with Jean working with him shoulder to shoulder. It's funny, and I hate to admit it, but my memories tend to revolve around myself. Lee's friends were much younger and Mike's were older. I never had very close friends. Everybody was my friend. I would visit friends with my bike or sometimes I'd go to the Museum and watch Peter and Jean work. The Ringling was (and still is) quite palatial. Lots of

marble, arches, and baroque architecture built
around a beautiful multi-terraced garden full
of sculptures. In front was a large bull in wild
movement with a naked lady strapped on its
back. Straight out the back were more gardens,
the Oslo Theater, lots of lawn, and huge banyan
trees. Next-door was the Ringling Mansion with
a large marble landing with steps going to the
Sarasota Bay. Standing among it all was a life-
sized, bronze replica of Michelangelo's "David."

Fall arrived and it was time to fiberglass and
paint the boat. This had to be done with the boat
in a tilted position so the bottom was accessible.
When one side was done, it would be tilted the
other way to do the other side. The boat was
very heavy. Tilting it would require as many
bodies as possible, so we had tilting parties. All
the neighbors had been watching the building
of the boat and they seemed to get a kick out of
helping. At night, we talked about what it would
be like to sail the West Indies. When the time
came to launch the Simplicity (so named because
even a boy could sail it by himself even though
it was 36 feet long and 15 feet wide) all of Peter
and Jean's friends were there. Jean smashed
the champagne on the bow and proclaimed,
"I christen thee Simplicity." And there she
was—like a beautiful living creature floating in

the most gracious manner. Our first mooring was out in the back of the museum. We were supposed to go there after school finished and get on our boat for her maiden voyage: we were going to Madeira Beach to install a one-cylinder motor, built in 1908 but never used.

What a delight to see Eric Von Schmidt on the boat! Then It was almost sunset, and Mike still hadn't shown up. Peter expressed his disappointment that we weren't more excited about this new adventure. Eric was one of the great folk singers at the time and he sang songs while Jean fixed dinner. Afterwards, gliding across the Tampa Bay reminded me of the Dolphin Dance a few years before. Eric was singing about the "Ee-ri-ee Canal (as opposed to the Erie Canal) and I was looking up at the stars and thinking about Jean Williams.

Earlier, when Mike had finally shown up, Peter again mentioned his disappointment in our lack of excitement about this maiden voyage of the Simplicity. Mike's excuse was that he had been saying his last good-byes to his friends.

He said to me, "Hey Pat, I saw Jean Williams."

I said "Oh yeah?"—thinking about how I really hadn't had a chance to say good-bye to her.

"Yeah, she was really sad that you were going

and said to give you this bracelet to remind you of her." He handed me a chrome bracelet with a plaque that said 'Jean.' What a romantic notion.

As I was looking up at the stars and thought how people touch one another's hearts as we make this journey through life, led on by some magical mystery always beyond our reach, yet close enough to keep going toward the stars of our dreams and visions. So many extraordinary things had happened to the five of us as a result of one man thinking, "I'm a young man who has seen and tasted the best and worst in life, let my guiding perspective and goal revolve around, or go straight toward, the best, toward the beauty, the creativity of life and the doing of *that*, rather than someone else's program," and taking his wife and children along with him. There was part of us boys that rebelled against it. There was a part of us that wanted to be like everybody else. This never really completely went away, no matter how much we realized we were having experiences very few of our contemporaries would ever have.

Soon we were back in Madeira Beach, aboard the Simplicity, near St. Petersburg, where we had lived before on the Melody after selling the Sandpiper. This is where we installed the aforementioned "Maria," a one-cylinder motor of certain antiquity, yet like new. After renewing our old acquaintances, a couple of days later we were on our way to the West Indies.

It was the end of 1958, beginning of 1959. Winter in the sub-tropics. Storm season. Halfway between Sarasota and Naples, Florida, about ten miles out at sea, a fierce storm brewed up. It was night and we boys were down below while Peter and Jean guided the boat through the waves that would come crashing down. The sails were reefed (the bottoms tied up to make them smaller for better control). Most of the time Peter was able to make the boat plane across the waves, but sometimes the Simplicity would come crashing down with a large "BOOM" at the bottom and she would shake so bad it seemed like one more time and she would fall apart. This went on for what seemed like all night with Peter and Jean up there in their foul weather gear and corn-cob pipes turned upside down so they could smoke them without getting water in their pipes.

My Father

My father Peter Krohn,
Master of the seas,
A builder of wooden boats,
A painter of vision,
For and by the human being,
Their forms carefully and lovingly
Narrated by the ocean herself.
Son of Neptune,
At his best when she rises up!
In a tempest, so wild and demanding,
Only those she chooses
Survive her heaving breasts,
And the chasms of her great womb.
Only that boat she knows
As her daughter
Will experience the tranquility
After *that* storm.
When the jester,
That subtly and not so subtly,
Is played out, and goes to His home,
And the ever-abiding consciousness
Of satori quietly ushers in,
A schism so great,
A new being comes through,
The absolute,
Ineffable glory of creation unfolds,

All seas become navigable,
And adventures follow.
Peter doesn't talk much anymore,
And *that*, yes *that* is Why.

By morning the storm had passed. The
sun came out and we were all up on deck
sailing toward Naples, the last town before the
Everglades at that time. From there, we would
cut across the Gulf of Mexico to Key West. In
Naples, Peter gave the Simplicity a going over to
make sure she had weathered the storm intact,
reorganizing and checking the rigging and
anything else that may have been affected by
the storm. The next day we were on our way to
Key West. As we headed out of the mooring in
Naples, Maria was going Pa-ca-Pa-ca-Pa-ca-Pa-
ca as she cheerfully powered us slowly out to sea
where we would set sail.

17 Florida Keys

I was almost twelve years old. At that age life
changes don't seem so profound, or maybe it
just seems that way because we were such rolling
stones. We were headed for a life of adventure
predetermined only by the blowing of the wind
and the pull of exotic destinations. We had each
other and the Simplicity. Other than the clothes
in my bag, all I owned were my baseball cards
and books, baseball mitt and my bracelet from
Jean Williams, which soon disappeared because
of a life-long propensity to shed jewelry in
mysterious ways which still defies understanding.

From the tip of Florida, the Keys curve
south and westward through the Florida Straits.
Instead of following the west coast and the
curve of the keys, we went straight across the
Gulf of Mexico and Florida Straits, approaching
Key West from the open sea. One night out
at sea the fog was so thick that you couldn't
even see the water or even one-third the length
of the boat. This creates a unique form of
apprehension, almost like claustrophobia. Jean
must have felt it. Not knowing if everybody else
sensed the danger, she decided to dramatize it,

"I hope nobody fell overboard. If they did we might never find them."

I hadn't really thought about that and it suddenly occurred to all of us how ominous this thick fog was. I'm sure Peter was concerned that an approaching large boat or ship might not see our running lights until it was too late. Suddenly, with a sickening fear-induced sound in her voice, Jean yelled out "Where's Mike? I don't see Mike anywhere." For what seemed like minutes we wondered if Mike had disappeared into some imagined abyss as we checked on each other looking for Mike and yelling, "Mike! Mike! Mike!"

Deciding it was time to allay our suffering, he popped up out of the foc'sle (up in the bow were we boys slept) and yelled back, "I'm up forward."

Relieved but shaken Jean replied, "You scared the hell out of me! Alright, let's all stay together until this fog lifts."

We basically drifted all night. In the morning we continued sailing toward Key West under clear skies. When we came in sight of the Keys, the water became shallow and treacherous. We could see the bottom through the clear water. Much of it was sandy but there were rocky reefs and no channel markers until we got a lot closer. So the sails came down and we

poled for miles, while Peter looked out up in
the bow for obstacles that could tear a hole in
the bottom of the Simplicity. Of course, with
the lightness of the wood construction and
the toughness of the fiberglass in tandem, the
Simplicity would most likely glance off without
damage at such a slow speed. However, Peter
was not one to underestimate the treachery
of a reef. Meanwhile, there was much visual
fascination as we passed over the myriad forms
of sea life. Many different kinds of seaweed were
swaying with the movement of the water as little
fish darted and big fish glided with graceful
movements, and whole schools of fish moved in
unison in the quickness of a moment.

Soon we were following channel markers with
our sails up as we got closer to Key West. First
we passed the naval base with all its cruisers,
ships and submarines and sailors waving. There
among the grey vessels was a pink submarine!

"That's the funniest shade of undercoat I've
ever seen,"surmised Peter, "and the strangest
thing is that they put her in the water like that."
It turned out that they were filming a Tony
Curtis and Janet Leigh movie called "Operation
Petticoat." It was a comedy where they had to
resurrect this battle weary submarine and only
had pink paint for the job. My guess is that it

was during the making of that film that at least the idea of Jamie "Lee" Curtis was conceived, if not Ms. Curtis herself.

One night Jean came home from working at a very fine Italian restaurant named Luigi's in Key West, where we were docked in a Marina, and told us about Tony Curtis and Janet Leigh coming into the restaurant. "The two of them were so profoundly beautiful and perfect looking it was almost unreal." It seems true beauty in life is generally an ephemeral perception, so much so that the constant beauty that is to be experienced in our lives many times goes by unnoticed. Maybe we're too busy to notice. Because of our previous associations with Cubans in Mexico City, we had developed a fondness for the culture, the people, the music, food, coffee and their spirit, which is both fiery and peaceful, with a cultural sophistication that has always intrigued me. There was a civil war going on in Cuba, as Castro was in the midst of wresting power from the long-standing dictator, Batista. Consequently, there were many Cuban refugees in Key West. The schools were conducting double sessions to accommodate all the new children, including nautical gypsies like us three boys. There were also many Cuban men walking around in olive green fatigues looking every bit

like Castro, with beards, cigars and the rest. I
assume this was a ruse to conceal the real Castro,
unless it was a preview of the Elvis Syndrome in
Las Vegas.

In the midst of all this it was obvious that
these were dangerous waters, so we sold the boat
to friends for basically what it cost to build:
$1,000 down, $500 later. That was a nice stash
of cash in 1959, so first, we took a bus to Miami
and then we took a plane to Mexico City. We
had a free apartment to stay in. Mexico was still
pretty much the way we remembered it. While
Peter and Jean looked up their old friends and
went dancing at night, we boys rediscovered the
city, riding buses, walking through the markets
and parks, playing baseball and generally having
a good time.

At night, we would listen to records and read.
I found a book called "The Billie Holiday Story."
It was my first grown up book and, at 12 years
old, I guess I was ready for it because I found it
fascinating. In Key West at night, I would lie in
the cabin listening to a record featuring Billie
Holliday, Ella Fitzgerald, Lena Horne and Anita
O' Day. I never tired of hearing that record,
so I thoroughly enjoyed reading the ups and
downs, ins and outs of her life in the jazz world.
The people, the whorehouses and what went on

in those places, the jazz clubs, the South, the North, the East, West, New York, New Orleans, and other big cities, and the drugs, alcohol, and the jazz people that didn't dabble in those things. I was curious about marijuana, but from the way Billy Holliday's life went, I didn't want any part of heroin or anything like it.

After a couple of weeks in Mexico City, we were on our way back to the USA. We got on a night train to Guadalajara. "We want you boys to know what it's like to sleep in a Pullman before the modern world completely phases them out and they become a thing of the past," explained Peter. This was their gift to us – forever exposing us to experiences that would shape our perceptions of the world, and memories we would cherish.

The trip started out like any other. We boys faced each other on couch-like benches and Jean and Peter had a separate compartment much the same, watching the nighttime scenery go by. Then at ten o'clock the seats were converted into a bed, the curtains to the aisle were drawn and we fell asleep to the clickety clack of the metal wheels on the tracks, as we continued watching the shadow scenes through the windows. Before we left Mexico City, the whole family had gone to a showing of the James Dean, Liz Taylor, Rock

Hudson movie, "Giant." Early on, Rock Hudson and Liz Taylor slept in a Pullman while traveling to Texas. Maybe that's what gave our parents the idea. Perhaps they had never traveled in a Pullman together either.

In any case, we woke up in the morning approaching Guadalajara. We spent a day and night in Guadalajara checking out the sites, shopping for chalecos (Mexican jacket-vests made from a thick cotton weave to keep warm) and hanging out with the Mariachis in the restaurant district, where they could be found by the hundreds.

We arrived in San Diego on a quiet Sunday morning. The day was sunny and poetically beautiful and we were in high spirits—but we were broke. The good news was that we had an ace in the hole. Peter and Jean's friends in Key West still owed us $500 from the boat. Peter got on the phone in hopes of getting some money wired to us. I could tell something was very wrong by the tone of the conversation. Apparently Bob Kaufman (a different person than the "beat" poet we knew in Woodstock) had been smoking in bed and his house burned down with him in it. Of all our Key West friends, he was our favorite. A pleasant and cheerful soul, he was a real gentleman, a wonderful man, from a very wealthy family with a chain of jewelry stores based in New York. Peter and Jean had turned him on to marijuana and apparently he became very stoned and nodded off. We were still a young family and this was the first death of anyone that was close to us.

18 Back to San Francisco

When the money came, we got on a bus to San Francisco to start a new life. I always tried to get a seat in the very front because you could see more and experience the feeling of transport, that mysterious magic of traveling through time and space. By the time we got started it was late in the day, so we would be traveling through the night.

I sat next to an enjoyable middle-aged lady who seemed excited about traveling too. "Where are you folks going?" she asked.

"San Francisco," I replied.

"Oh, that's a great city, I love San Francisco" she exclaimed!

I told her I was born there and this was my first time going back. "I don't even remember it because I was only a year old when we left. Are you going to San Francisco too?" I asked.

"Oh no," she said. "This time I'm going to Zheecago, that's how we pronounce Chicago, just like people in San Francisco say Frisco, or instead of Los Angeles, L.A."

"That's interesting," I thought, suddenly feeling worldly and educated.

In those days traveling was mostly highway with a lot of stops and towns, and I made the observation that places were like people, certain attributes in common, yet each one different and unique in its own way. Basically we would go from the highway to the town's main street, stopping at the bus stop. It was sometimes just a bench in front of a store, and other times a small building that might be old art deco, modern, or nondescript cinder-block architecture, but always there was the blue dog in neon light. Some towns had a racial mixture, but others had only so called "white" people, which I thought was weird because I thought California was integrated. Sometimes Main Street was just the part of town the highway passed through. At night you mostly saw people of all kinds, yet with one common thread, they were people in between destinations; maybe just across the street, or down the block, or across town, or like us, a whole cross-country life transition, making discoveries, saying "How do you do?" to the next circumstance of life.

San Francisco has always been my favorite of all big cities. I had always known that someday we would return, and I was very excited that we had done so. Spring starts early on the California coast. By the time we arrived in March, spring was in full swing. Perfect Spring days in San Francisco are euphorically beautiful. Blue skies, puffy clouds, colorful people, cars, archtecture, and all set on hills that give a sense of accessibility and smallness to the neighborhoods. When we got off the bus near Market Street (which is the main drag in downtown San Francisco) we took the trolley to a cable car that would take us into North Beach.

We got off the cable car near Columbus Street, just past Broadway, which is where North Beach begins. The North Beach Public Library was nearby, with a playground, tennis court, and a large area for softball, with the baseball diamonds all set into the hillside. Kids could play fast-pitch, a game consisting of a wall, a home plate painted on the blacktop and a strike zone painted on the wall. From a rubber-painted "mound" on the blacktop, you tried to strike out the batter with a tennis ball.

Mike, Lee, and I hung out and watched the bags, while Peter and Jean went looking for a place to rent. It was an interesting place to sit and watch the world coming and going around us. There was an intersection of cultures where we sat at the edge of the Italian community, with China Town just a few blocks away and the black section just over the hill. The Mission or Mexican district was way over on the other side of Market Street, but this was an area where there was a mixture of many cultures.

Eventually Peter and Jean came back and we went to our new residence—the Colombo Hotel. It was on the corner of Broadway and Grant, within a block of Columbus and Kearney, the City Lights Book Store, Chinatown, the bohemian scene on Grant Street, and the Jazz Workshop. We had a window on the second floor that looked out over Grant Street in Chinatown.

In the morning we went to our new school. Mike went to Francisco Jr. High and Lee and I went to Garfield Elementary. I was very amazed to find almost all the children at the school were Chinese. In my class of more than thirty students, only three of us were not Chinese, and the three of us sat together, which at the time felt natural. The other two were both Mexican. Carlos was a little smaller than me and the other, Joaquin, was much bigger than me. The first chance I got I asked his name and he said "Wahkeen."

I said, "You mean like 'walking?'"

He said "yeah."

I thought, "Wow, even the Mexicans sound Chinese." In the playground we had recess and lunch. We were all required to bring a bag lunch. Jean always made us sandwiches and we'd buy 1/3-pint containers of milk for 10 cents.

Joaquin was kind of a good-natured tough guy. Carlos was gentler and also good-natured. He liked my chaleco. He said "I know that's Mexican, what's it called?"

"It's a chaleco," I told him.

"That's pretty cool," he said admiringly. There was another boy that I would see in the playground, Robin, who had blond hair. We were the only two blonds in school. I only made playground friends, which was okay because I never felt a need to make a close friend. After all, I was different. Eventually, it became obvious to all of them that I was different. One day Carlos, Joaquin, and Robin cornered me and asked, "Are you a beatnik?" The beats were the new cultural subdivision on the block. When we moved here a lot of Peter and Jean's old friends from Greenwich Village and Woodstock had moved here, and Herb Caen of the San Francisco Chronicles had called the resulting sub cultural groundswell "Beatniks." This was because some of these new bohemians had written a collective Manifesto called "The Abomunist Manifesto," which delineated a way of nonconformist life along the lines of the Classic Beatitudes, hence calling themselves "Beats" or "Beat."

So I was inclined to answer, "Yeah, I guess so."

That was followed by, "Are your parents beatniks too?"

"I guess you would call them that."

It all started with "Sputnik", the first satellite in outer space launched by man, in this case the Russians. The cold war was still very real and many people were very afraid of "the red Menace." Anything different from the American way of life was considered by many to be communistic; when in actuality the so-called "Beat" way of life (if there ever was a particular one) was the exact opposite, since communism requires conformity.

Joaquin said, "I hear from a friend that they could see beatniks across the way from his window walking around naked and fucking."

"Well I've never seen anything like that, and besides that, I'm pretty sure all grownups do that in private," I replied.

"You've never seen your parents do that?" asked Robin.

"Of course not!" I replied, trying to get myself back in the norm, after all I was still only twelve.

I think Joaquin was older than us, because he made us all laugh when he said, "Sure sounds like fun though!" As far as I was concerned, everybody now knew where he stood, and the beatnik issue was settled.

Still more interested in baseball than girls, I always liked to go to the North Beach playground and join in a softball game after school. One day, however, I found myself walking alongside a pretty Chinese girl from my class named Cynthia. "Hi Pat," she said. "You know my name don't you?"

I have never been good with names, so I guessed "Pam?"

"No, it's Cynthia, you sure are a kidder," she said with a giggle.

"Yeah, I was just kidding – Hi, Cindy."

"No—not Cindy – Cynthia!" she corrected. Cynthia was a very charming, likable girl. It turned out she was going to the library too. In the coming weeks we would walk together often, in fact we became best friends. We had a crush on each other, yet our relationship was never more than platonic.

Our old friend, Bob Kaufman from Woodstock days, always treated me like an old friend, and greeted me with excitement. "Hey Pat! What's happening?"

"I'm going to play softball." I replied.

"Crazy man! Someday I'm going to take you

to see Willy Mays play! That guy is amazing to watch!" he gesticulated.

"I'll bet," I said, thinking "Wouldn't that be great." Another old friend I'd see frequently was George Connolly. George air brushed helicopter parts for a living, but was a renaissance man of art, also dabbling in acting, spoken word and music. One day after I came home from school, he was hanging out with Peter and Jean sharing a big bowl of Bing cherries. I couldn't remember ever seeing real fresh cherries in Florida, Mexico or New Orleans, and my memories of New York didn't seem to have any, so that was really a treat.

We didn't have a kitchen, so more often than not we would go to a Chinese restaurant for dinner and order three dishes that always came with rice and fortune cookies, preceded by a complimentary bottomless pot of tea, so the whole family could eat out for three to four dollars.

Jean and Peter had brought back a one-pint jar of Mexico's best 'Acapulco Gold' marijuana, so they were very popular among their friends, and were doing a lot of socializing and generally having a good time. We boys went to school, played softball and walked around North Beach and Chinatown, taking in the sights and activities going on around us. City Lights bookstore was like a library and you could spend hours there. I never did because my reading at that time was anything about baseball and that was it, but there was something alluring about the small spaces filled with what seemed like interesting books, and the people they attracted. That being said, I had found the Billie Holiday book interesting, and was developing a pedestrian interest in books other than baseball, although when Ginsburg wrote about masturbating in the shower, I thought, "Why would someone write about that?"

San Francisco people were so many and varied. I never stopped being fascinated with different bohemians. They really weren't the stereotypes the various media made them out to be, they had ethnic clothing and looks from all over the world, especially Europe. Many had beards of all kinds, but many didn't. They were Chinese, Italian, Greek, Jewish and more. Chinatown was very colorful, much as it is today, but less modern, with exotic smells and sounds, people talking and yelling at each other in Chinese and of course, tourists from all over the world. Even outside of Chinatown, most of the little grocery stores (and there were a lot) were Chinese, but on the beach side of Broadway the stores were quieter because of the Italian presence.

Grant Street was where the Beats congregated, on that side of Broadway where the Italian coffee houses, delicatessens and little Chinese stores existed side by side. There the neighborhood energy and character was bohemian on the wild side, unlike the more genteel bohemian coffee house next to the City Lights bookstore. The Grant Street coffee houses, except for the more sedate, very European Italian ones, would be crowded with Beats digging jazz, art, folk music, blues, poetry and each other. It was a wild, crazy scene, especially after the sun went down.

One day "Jungle Jim," as he was called because of the safari hat he wore, rode by on his Harley Davidson motorcycle. "Hi Pat, have you seen Phyllis?" he boomed out. (Jungle Jim was a big guy, and unless he was in a conversation his voice would usually boom.)

"I think she and George are meeting us over at the Colombo and then we're gonna have Chinese," I returned.

"Hey, check it out man, I found this far out tea in a crazy little store in Chinatown," he said as he peeled a square paper package out of his saddlebag. "It's called Wo Hop Gon Jim tea; Gone Jim! That's me!"

"Wow, man, you're even a legend in China," I joked.

"I wouldn't be surprised, they call me "Jaime de la Selva" in Mexico," he bragged. Jungle Jim was one of those guys who was a walking, talking event. He was actually a tourist attraction.

The beat scene was actually such an anarchistic collection of self-created characters, how could anybody be called "King of the Beats." It was too wild and crazy for that. There was "Hube the Cube" – the original Harwood Alley beat poet, with his beret and goatee and brooding personality. There was "Bigness" – a tall, lanky guy with a scruffy beard, with bell bottoms like an English sailor, who always acted like a big scene was ready to happen or he was going to create one. "Madness" had a Greco-Roman haircut with short hair combed forward. He exuded a kind of reverential madness, with a constant wide-eyed expression, but he was also called "Paris" because he played a beautiful flute and was prone to present a Greek god-like appearance. There were the conga players like Joaquin Murietta (naming himself after the famous Mexican Robin Hood), an excellent conga player and intellectual man-about-town. And on and on – one character after another.

Stan Kenton's band had a permanent gig on the corner of Columbus and Broadway, opposite our hotel in a dinner/nightclub with open arches on the Columbus side. I used to walk by on the way home from the park and stop to listen to the great sounds of that band. If I walked up Grant, there would be a couple of coffees houses that held conga battles. With those guys it was all about power and speed, which was a whole other kind of expression than the Afro-Cuban percussionists I was used to hearing; very much like the difference between speed skating and figure skating. Caribbean dancers demand much more variety and feeling and the musicians comply with countless types of polyrhythms based on melody or, more often than not, melodies based on rhythm, constantly inventing new combinations and patterns.

At the height of spring, the street was closed off for several blocks for the Grant Street Celebration. They had a bandstand playing jazz, folk music and blues. A modern dance group danced in and out of the crowds with calypso drums. There was a beard contest, arts and crafts, and just a whole lot of people eating, drinking, celebrating, and just enjoying the vibe.

I ran into Ray the Barber, as he was digging the soprano sax player. The soprano was shaped like a small alto instead of the elongated one made famous by Coltrane and Bechet. Ray the Barber was a classic hipster – always dressed in good-looking clothes, yet bohemian looking with a well-trimmed beard. He had a barber shop over a triangular corner at Kearney Street, one block down from Broadway in a Victorian-style building, taking full advantage of the acute corner, creating a very attractive architectural style with curved glass and ornate trim. Many times I would walk by, look up and see him cutting hair by the window on the second floor, and we would sometimes wave at each other. He was a successful Mexican American. He had found his niche, as they say. Sometimes I would see him at the North Beach playground playing tennis in his "whites."

So Ray was there, in a khaki outfit with shorts, enjoying the jazz and the street fair. We exchanged greetings, "Hi Pat,"

"Hi Ray."

"How's the folks," he asked?

"They're okay!" I said and then volunteered, "They're probably at George's." George Connolly had a really nice pad tucked away in an apartment house mostly occupied by Chinese on a very steep section of Kearny, just above Broadway. You could usually tell if he was home because his VW bug would be parked outside (which was really a cool thing to have in those days.) After accessing the main hall, Phyllis and Jungle Jim's pad was on the right, and then you would walk to the very end to a very small courtyard (ten feet by ten feet). Looking up, there was a skylight about four stories above. You could identify George's pad by the rice paper in the windows with palmate Japanese maple leaves incorporated into the paper. I always like to visit his pad. He had teakwood soy sauce barrels made into drums with Yin Yang symbols on top. Being an artist, he set off his oriental motif with a mural he painted on the wall, of a long, gnarly cherry tree branch with well-placed cherry blossoms. But what really set it off was that he used gold leaf exclusively to define the branch. It was a very hip pad.

George was one of my favorite beat characters. When Peter and Jean first met him as an art student in Woodstock and Greenwich Village, he had a big bushy beard, but he had since shaved it off because he enjoyed playing different characters in his spare time. He could have been a very good actor. Sometimes he put on a fedora and black suit and hung out with the old Italians that looked like Cosa Nostra members in Columbus Park. Inevitably, they would try speaking Italian with him, to which he would reply, "Perdona, I no longer speak Italiano, when I lefta the olda country, I said when I geta to

America, I speaka the new language of the new country." After all, he didn't want to be one of them, he just wanted to hang out and pretend for a while. Other times he would put on his tweed suit and his "Robbie" hat, also made of English tweed and go to Chinatown and pretend he was an English gent, and play variations of this game as well.

Getting back to Ray the Barber and me digging jazz at the street fair, Ray said, "I'd go and enjoy some of that Acapulco Gold with George, Peter and Jean, but I have a one o'clock appointment to cut somebody's hair." Ray was not a regular barber. He gave razor cuts that shortened a person's hair, but made it look so natural that it didn't look like they had just had a haircut. He was very expensive.

My brother Mike was bragging about the money he was making selling newspapers down by the wharf, so I asked him to see if he could get a corner for me to sell newspapers also. I was in luck! A boy on the corner of Van Ness and Polk was quitting and I could have his corner, so at 3 PM every day I was selling the Call-Bulletin at Van Ness and Polk.

On a hot summer day, while selling papers, I was listening to the Giants baseball game on my transistor radio that I had bought for a dollar.

A new rookie named Willie McCovey had just come up from the minors and been put into the lineup at first base. One of the greatest first basemen of all time was already playing there, namely Orlando Cepeda. Either McCovey or Cepeda was playing outfield – I can't remember – unless Cepeda was hurt, but every time McCovey came up he got a hit. I think it was two triples and two singles. Standing on the corner selling newspapers and telling everybody about the new star, since baseball was the most important thing to me at that time, I felt I was experiencing and sharing history being made then and there.

The next thing I knew it was summer and time for change again. "We're moving to Noe Valley!" Jean exclaimed. Peter and Jean had found a very reasonable abode in a business section of Noe Valley on Castro Street, where Peter could have a cabinet shop and we could live in the back. Peter was going to make fine teakwood office furniture, especially desks for high-end offices. In order to keep my paper job, I had to take a bus to Mission Street, where I would transfer to a trolley to take me to Market Street, where I then transferred to a cable car that dropped me off one block from my corner. It was too far to go and they wanted somebody closer, so that job didn't last much longer.

One day Jean said Brew Moore (a new friend
of Peter and Jean's that they had met in San
Francisco) was going on a cruise and his wife
would like me to stay with them while he was
gone. Brew was a fine tenor saxophone player
who was one of the progenitors of what came to
be known as "West Coast Jazz."

"Would you like to do that?" she said, "They
have a TV." Television was a novelty to me so it
sounded like fun. They had a little girl (I think
she was 7 or 8) and Brew's wife had a part-time
day job, so we would stay home, play games
and watch TV. It was kind of fun seeing how
"normal" people lived, but I was glad to have my
freedom back when it was over.

One morning, George Connolly came by with
a very beautiful young couple. She was a gorgeous
redhead named Barbara with a melodic southern
accent, totally charming. Her husband's name
was Mike, and was a very likable guy. Mike and
Barbara were scientists. They both worked for
Lockheed-Martin. She was a mathematician and
he was a physicist, and they were both think-tank
analysts. Their relationship with Peter and Jean
followed the pattern of interesting people with
whom they became friends, including doctors,
lawyers, architects, clergy, museum directors,
marine biologists, aviation engineers, inventors,

boat or nautical people, teachers, psychologists, psychiatrists, athletes, and other people outside the bohemian world that enjoyed spending time with them, exchanging ideas and good times. People were always coming by just to hang out and talk and watch Peter work. Peter loved everything about woodworking, starting with the way it looked, smelled and felt in his hands.

"Working with wood is an act of love," he would say. "Everything you do with it is a caress or special movement that reflects your heart and soul, and that of the tree from which it came." He would talk about the differences between softwoods and hardwoods, and softwoods and softwoods, and hardwoods and hardwoods, and the uniqueness within kinds. "Here, smell the difference between sugar pine and ponderosa – the sweetness is almost intoxicating."

Our life was about deeper meanings and understandings that could not be realized unless you took the time to see beyond the platitudes and common denominator appeals.

On some weekends we would go to Mike and Barbara's home in the coastal range, up behind Redwood City. George would come and get us and take us in his VW bug. Once we needed coats, so we stopped at a Salvation Army thrift shop. I found a beautiful blue suede jacket that was seven dollars, which was more than many people made in a day in the fifties. "Do you like that coat?" asked George.

"Yeah, but it's way too expensive," I replied.

"If it fits, I'll buy it for you," he said.

I thought about the girls that used to chase me around after I sang Elvis' "Blue Suede Shoes" and thought, "Wow, this is even cooler than the blue suede shoes I had always wanted."

Mike and Barbara's house was up in the Redwoods. It was small but had a large living room, and at night we would stake out our sleeping spots. It was very modern with windows facing the trees that made up 80% of the wall space, with large red-orange curtains, which were usually open during the day and closed at night.

The Krohn boys were explorers. Wherever we went, we were given the free run of our environs with the only limitations being where signs were posted, "Keep Out," or "No Trespassing." We would start with the deer trails. When we came to a road we would walk down it to see where it went, or until we saw an interesting trail, another road, and so forth, until we got hungry or it got late.

One time we came home with great big, gorgeous, delicious apples and Jean said, "Let's have baked apples!" Until then we had mostly lived in tropical or subtropical locations, so this was a new and intriguing experience for us.

19 Palo Alto

Meanwhile, Peter and Jean got a job restoring and building wooden sailboats in Palo Alto, so that was our next home. By now I was in seventh grade and for the first time I became more involved in football. I pulled a pass out of the air, against a number of opponents who were trying to intercept it, so the quarterback made me his go-to guy. My glory was short lived when I couldn't seem to repeat the accomplishment.

After school, however, there were always a bunch of guys that wanted to play at a field near our house. It turned out there was a black kid, Mickey, who lived nearby and became my best friend. The central California fall brought a lot of warm sunny days for playing football, and if we couldn't get enough guys together we'd play whiffle ball in the back yard. A whiffle ball is a baseball shaped plastic ball with numerous holes so it couldn't be thrown or hit very far or fast, and would float or break in unpredictable ways so it made for an interesting game in a small space. One day, Mickey and I were watching a football game on his television and we were talking about who the best athletes were. Mickey said, "Hey Pat, did you ever notice how the best athletes are black?"

I replied, "I hadn't really thought about it before, but do you really think so?"

After which he rolled off "J.D. Smith, R.C. Owens, Jimmy Brown," and on and on.

I said "Yeah, but what about Y.A. Title, John Unitas, and Paul Hornung?" (Those were some of the super stars back then.)

"Alright, but there are so many more good black ones." I had never thought along those lines because one of the reasons we had moved away from Florida was so that we boys would have more interracial exposure, and I had never really considered how important this issue might be to him because he was black and blacks were a minority.

I didn't care too much for the notion that my race (I didn't know about my great-great black grandmother at the time) was somehow inferior, but I could see that this was very important to him, so I said "It sounds like you know more about this than I do, so you're probably right."

"Damn right I'm right," he said.

"Okay, then let's play some whiffle ball," I said, deciding we had pretty much exhausted the subject.

When we got downstairs he said, "Let me play my favorite record for you."

"Cool" I responded. It was "Venus" by Frankie Avalon. I noticed all the furniture in the living room had a thick plastic cover. In fact the whole house and yard was as neat as a pin. I couldn't help but think that in some ways he was more white than me, yet fiercely loyal to his black heritage. Still, we had a very comfortable friendship.

In the middle of the song, his father came home and wanted to talk to him privately, so while they talked in the kitchen, I sat on the plastic-covered couch and listened to Frankie Avalon. Presently he returned and said, "We've got tickets to the Stanford game, you wanna come?"

I said, "Yeah, that'd be great." Palo Alto is where Stanford University is. I guess his father was some kind of a professional and they were pretty well off, because his father was a booster for the 49'ers and *knew* J.D. Smith and R. C. Owens. Sometime in the following week I went by Mickey's house and he was throwing the football with a big black guy in the driveway.

"Hi Pat, can you guess who I'm playing catch with?"

In my head I thought, "That looks like J.D. Smith," but suffering from incredulity I said, "No."

"It's J.D. Smith," then, "J.D., this is my friend, Pat."

Kind of awed I managed a "Pleased to meet you" and shook his hand. We played catch for a while and talked about football.

The Dodgers played the Chicago White Sox in the World Series that year. The Dodgers' ace that year (in spite of Don Drysdale and the as yet unheralded Sandy Koufax) was a young kid named Larry Sherry who won two games. The White Sox ace was Early Wynn, a 39 year old veteran who had had a remarkable year, for once, playing with a winning team after playing for the Washington Senators for almost twenty years, winning some 300 games and losing almost as many. Peter and Jean were doing pretty well so we had a great Christmas that year and got a basketball, baseball gloves, and really nice baseball bats.

20 Heading South

Not very far into the New Year we were moving
to Santa Barbara where Peter was going to build
trimarans. Trimarans are sailboats with a main
hull and a small hull on either side, and they're
supposed to be more stable and faster than
Catamarans. So the next thing you know, we're
on a bus going down the coast a little over 200
miles to Santa Barbara, still with nothing more
than the bags on our backs, baseball gloves and
bats. We arrived early on an overcast morning,
stored our bags at the bus station and walked
down State Street (main street, Santa Barbara)
to the pier and out onto the pier. From there,
you could see the whole city built on foothills
leading down to the beach. On one side was the
marina with numerous boats docked together
like sardines, and on the other side boats were
moored in the bay where they danced on the
waves.

Our friends in Santa Barbara were Girard
and Angeli and their two children (a baby and
a toddler). Girard was an artist and a musician
who played an incredible saxophone, but at this
time he was working in construction. Girard

had a bright, energetic personality that made you feel like the moments of life were filled with incredible joy. Angeli was one of those classic beauties that you rarely meet and even more rarely call a friend. She was so sweet and kind and the kind of person that always seemed to find the common ground in conversation. Besides being the perfect mother and friend, I don't know what her creative outlets were. Maybe she was a poet or writer.

Once we figured out the way to their house, we found there was a city bus that would take us to within three blocks of the bus stop out in Goleta. I guess the plan was to stay with them until we got our own place. It wasn't too hard to find the house once we got out there. Most of the neighborhood had been leveled except for a few houses here and there. We boys were in luck! There was a high school nearby with plenty of basketball courts and athletic fields.

When we got to the house and knocked on the door, we received a very warm greeting. Once inside we found not only Girard and Angeli and their children, but also some friends from San Francisco; Nick (the Greek) Bonopolis, his wife Beverly and their first child, and his sister Cleo, who was pregnant. With the five of us Krohns, it was one full two-bedroom house! Funny thing is, I don't have any memories of feeling crowded or unwelcome.

One day Nick was taking me for a ride in his car and he asked me "Pat, do you like jazz?"

"I love jazz," I replied.

"Oh yeah? Which song comes to mind?"

I never really analyzed my likes and dislikes before so this was new territory for me. Then I remembered how we used to march around and dance to "When the Saints go Marchin' In" by Louis Armstrong, and offered that up. "How do you sing that song?" I proceeded to sing what I could remember, including the line, "I want to be in that number."

"That was okay", Nick said, "but in jazz, you're supposed to give the music your own twist – like 'I want to be in *that there* number. That's the beauty of jazz; it's always improvised to one degree or another, so that you express your own creative spirit."

That seemed challenging to me, and besides it seemed like an oddball notion. At any rate, it was an ideal I wasn't quite ready for. Nick wasn't sure if he was getting through, so he asked, "So what do you think about that, Pat?"

Well, I'm not sure," I answered, not knowing quite what to say. "But it sounds interesting," I added hoping to sound halfway intelligent.

"Sounds like I gave you something to think about," Nick said. He was a very interesting guy, and I always enjoyed listening to what he had to say, but I can remember feeling a little uncomfortable being mentally challenged about music, which I always felt was something to be enjoyed. To this day, I have always felt the mental aspect of it was overly challenging. However, over the years I have come to perceive and enjoy improvisation as anything but mental, more like the free form dancing I was exposed to, and absorbed by, in the Yucatan days. I did like the idea that a grown-up I liked was bouncing ideas off my head. It was uncharted territory.

At night, early in the evening, some of the jazz musicians from a Santa Barbara nightclub called, "The Boom-Boom," would come by, hang out and play congas in a mellow tone.

Angeli said "Hey Pat, did you know Tiny's a professional conga player? Tiny—show Pat how to play." Actually Tiny was a really big guy with a very gentle disposition who was playing with tones that were both rhythmic and melodic and very enjoyable.

"Well, the first thing you have to learn is Momma-Daddy." He demonstrated, playing the four beats as he pronounced the four syllables, and that was my first and only conga lesson.

One of the first things we did as soon as we arrived was to start school. In order to get to school I had to cross a ravine behind our house where the railroad tracks ran, and catch a bus on the other side that would go to La Colina Jr. High School. I was enrolling in the middle of the winter quarter, so I got a lot of special attention during the orientation process. It was a brand new school that had just been finished that year. The gym teacher explained how the hot water pipes ran under the floor in the locker room so the floors would never be cold, and somebody showed me where all my classes were, how to operate the combination on my lock, and so forth – all of which was very exciting.

Thirteen is an interesting age. One becomes, to some degree, an adult in the sense of individual perspective. You begin to get more of a handle on life in some of its more immediate aspects, while the adult world is still much bigger than you are. Everything is so new in a different way. At thirteen, you are on the edge of the cup of life not even thinking of being immersed in its contents, yet it's all there, new school, new friends, new place, new experiences. When it came to dancing I wasn't shy, but so many others were that it wasn't as much fun as with Jean Williams and the others when I was eleven.

So, I became the icebreaker and, as a result, I
was invited to a birthday party, which I was
unable to attend. The next day one of the boys
approached me and asked why I wasn't at the
birthday party. He said that when you are invited
to a party you should go, and that I had hurt the
birthday girl's feelings. I had never been aware
of social responsibility before. When I saw her
I apologized. I wouldn't let that happen again, I
thought. I never did. I've always had an aversion
to conflict and to hurt feelings, my own or those
of others.

One of the exciting things that happened in
Goleta at that time was a Bud Shanks/Shorty
Rogers concert at the San Marcos High School
just a few blocks away. I would return twenty-
five years later and catch the Count Basie
Orchestra being lead by Thad Jones (a couple
of years after the Count passed on), but that's
another story.

Eventually we moved into Santa Barbara to a
little old house at 409 Bath Street. There, Peter
built trimarans in the front yard. In those days
the freeway ended in Goleta and started up again
in Montecito. The part of the State Highway that
went through Santa Barbara was the old Camino
Real, just a two-lane highway that dated back
to Spanish Colonial times. Now Bath Street is

blocked from the beach by the Freeway, but then we could walk down to the beach on Bath Street, named for the spa that had been there at one time, but was now just a group of shallow pools.

One day my brother Mike said "Hey, Pat, there's a dance at the Carillo Auditorium."

"You mean like the Youth Center back in Sarasota?" I asked.

"Yeah, but it's a lot bigger."

"Sounds great! Count me in!" I told him.

Most of the attendees were African American or Mexican American and nobody I knew, but I didn't care. Everybody was dancing and having a good time. Almost everyone was jitterbugging (like swing except to a rock beat). "Cherry Pie" was a big hit then. Buddy Holly, Richie Valens and the Big Bopper were popular, having died in a plane crash a little over a year before. The Platters' "Harbor Lights" and "Misty" and "Red Sails in the Sunset" were the favorite slow dance songs. Every Friday night we would go and have a good time. A new thing for me was a couple of line dances called the "Hully Gully" and the "Slop." These were always initiated by tall Afro-American girls and involved rocking, shimmying and stroll-like steps.

I always danced with any willing female partner regardless of race or ethnic type, so

when a Mexican-American guy who was older
and bigger than me asked "How come you were
dancing with my girl?" I was quite off guard,
and when he sucker punched me in the face all
hell broke loose, as everybody started fighting in
defense of either him or me. I blacked out and
the next thing I knew some guys were putting
me in a '55 Chevy with "Chucos Crusos"
insignia on the side that looked like a cross with
pins radiating out from the center between the
bars. It was a Pachuco gang that was friends with
Mike. One of them said "It was a good thing we
got out of there before the cops arrived.

"Mike said, "You got jumped by some
Pachuco's, you okay?"

"Yeah, I'm okay" I replied, kind of in a state of
shock. Fighting was not something that existed
in my world. Mike, however, was the exact
opposite. He liked to associate with the "bad
guys" and was always welcomed as a friend or
ally by them, and was always known as "someone
you didn't mess with."

The "Carillo," as it was called, was closed
down after that, but about a week later on the
way home from baseball at the Boy's Club, the
same guys jumped me again. Before I could get
away they had bloodied my face pretty good,
and when I got home Peter and Jean flipped out

when they saw my face. They grabbed a hammer and a hatchet and went running down the street looking for the guys, but were stopped by a patrol car officer who wanted to know what was going on.

"Some Pachuco's beat my boy's face into a bloody pulp" (it turned out one of the Pachuco's had a snake ring on his finger which cut my face every time I was hit.)

"And if I find him I'm gonna kill him" yelled my mom.

"Settle down lady, let's see if we can find these guys, and meanwhile let's take your boy to the hospital."

Somehow they did find them and they came by the house and apologized. Unfortunately for them, now that Mike knew who they were they could not avoid a visitation of *his* wrath.

Summer was approaching and Peter finished his trimaran and for some reason it was time to move again. Peter was going to start painting again in Los Angeles. Before we left we enjoyed the apricots from the tree catty-corner to our house that were the best I remember before or since. I would climb up the tree every day and eat one after another as they ripened from day to day.

21 On the way to LA

By the time we got to Van Nuys, it was the middle of the night and we were trying to find the address of Bill and Donna Hood. They were old friends from the Mexico City College days as I mentioned earlier, with boys my and Lee's age, and a very young sister. The idea was to stay with them until we got our own place. Bill Hood had become a fine musician, composer, and arranger. He did B-movie studio work, like "Tarzan, Ape Man" with Steve Reeves, but he also worked with band leaders like Bill Holman and Marty Paitch, and other well-known jazz figures like "Red" Holloway, Shorty Rogers and Bud Shank. He had become a lesser-known but important member of the west coast jazz scene. They had a very nice ranch house with a pool in Van Nuys, which is smack dab in the middle of San Fernando Valley, home to bedroom communities for Hollywood and Los Angeles. By some kind of miracle we found their house in the middle of the night.

I have very fond memories of the two or three weeks we spent there. They also had an apricot tree in the back yard but we were told to eat

only a few as Donna was going to make apricot
wine. The days were spent keeping up with the
Dodgers after breakfast, swimming, playing
baseball, catching crawdads in the L.A. River
and otherwise exploring the environs. Mike had
stayed in Santa Barbara so he could hang with
his friends. I felt strange about that, but he was
now fifteen and Peter and Jean were okay with it,
and it was understood he would catch up with us
later.

We ended up in a part of L.A. called Silver
Lake, which was also the name of the huge
reservoir the neighborhoods were built around.

Blossom

Delicate beauty
Infinitely tiny source of wondrous beauty
Light gently bounces in its petals
And light glows out from within
Like an ancient song
That still charms the soul
Just like that
A blossom fell

A blossom that falls from a tree may leave
behind fruit or not. The blossoms that make
up the moments and certain generative periods

in our lives may also bring forth fruit or not. Sometimes blossoms simply are blossoms. Life is beautiful that way.

Through all the dreams, perils, tribulations and triumphs, the Krohns had seen their souls pass through. Peter and Jean were now in their mid-thirties with still only the bags on their backs. They had discovered that life is worth putting effort into, even though as the years go by it does get harder and one needs a place to rest and recuperate. This was a crossroads of sorts for us. Where do you go from here? How much longer can we just keep going and going? Not that these questions needed to be answered, but perhaps this was the first time they were even flirted with.

Peter and Jean were making the Hollywood scene. Conjure in your own mind what that may have meant, if you will. I'm sure there is abundant truth among all the clichés of who knows Holly-weird what. Read my mother's book. I'm sure there are truths in there that I'm not qualified to write about involving sex, drugs and all the rest.

I wasn't living in the adult world and didn't see much of my parents that summer. I was in the teenage world. I was having fun with friends I had made in the neighborhood. We went to the

Griffith Park Pool, and a trampoline park that stretched trampolines over holes in the ground so there was nowhere to fall. We played spin the bottle, (there was a pretty girl one year older named Vicky and when I got to kiss her I nearly flipped), and one night we all piled into an old jalopy and drove to Pacific Ocean Park where admission was only $1.50 and you could ride on the best rides all day; those kind of things.

I made friends with a guy my age who had a great way of making money selling first aid kits. "They sell for $1.25 and you get 25 cents for each one you sell."

I said, "Great! Count me in."

"But you have to learn the spiel," he added.

"What's a spiel?" I asked.

"A spiel is like a speech you memorize in order to get them to buy."

How does it go?" I asked.

"It goes like this – Hi, my name is Pat Krohn and I'm trying to earn my way to summer camp, and I have these great first aid kits that everyone should have in their home, or car, or at work in case of an emergency, and they're only $1.25."

That was easy. The next day a man, about 30 years old, picked us up with two or three other young guys. Most of the time we only made $5 or $6 and spent most of that at nice restaurants

he liked to take us to. One day I did make
$30.00, which was twice what the average adult
made in those days. Naturally, making all that
money made the summer more fun until one
day in Beverly Hills the cops took us all into the
precinct station. I remember one cop saying,
"These guys are all under age. What should we
do with him?"

"Book him!" was the reply. So we spent most
of the afternoon waiting for his girlfriend to
come and post bail.

22 Moving to Venice Beach

The summer was winding down. I had been staying with my friend, but then I got wind that Peter and Jean had found a place in Venice Beach on the ocean and that it was time for us all to reunite. It was the summer of 1960 and Eisenhower was still president. Jean had gotten a job in a coffee shop. "Guess who I waited on today?

"Who?"

"Victor Mature"

"What was he like?"

"He was just like in the movies – a real gentleman with a good sense of humor." She was glad to get a good tip – she said tips generally were not very good because it was an election year.

That summer, being a teenager, I was aware of the new hits like "Only the Lonely" by Roy Orbison, "Its Now or Never" by Elvis, "Diana" by Paul Anka, "I'm Sorry" by Brenda Lee, and they still played Oldies but Goodies like, "Little Darlin" by The Diamonds, and "I'm Walking to New Orleans" by Fats Domino, which we did the 'Stroll' to.

To get reunited at our new home, I got a ride to Century City, but ended up walking the rest of the way to Venice. Every once in a while, I would check my pocket for a ten-dollar bill, which was all I had left of my summer earnings. I didn't want to break it just to take the bus. I thought then at least I would have something to show Peter and Jean for my efforts. Long before I got to Venice, when I checked for it, it was gone.

Peter and Jean didn't really care if I had $10. They were just glad to see me. Apparently I was the only one not accounted for, so we were all back together for the first time since Santa Barbara.

This was the heyday of the Beat period in Venice and we had a beautiful 2nd floor flat right on Ocean Front Walk between Venice Blvd. and Washington St. In those days, there was still a section of the Boardwalk that was made of wood, between Venice Blvd. and us. Today there is a sandy isthmus ending at the rocky breakwater island about fifty yards out from the beach, but back then the 6000 square foot island was surrounded by water. Junior Lifeguards were required to swim around without stopping. The local population was dominated by beatniks and retired people. There were the muscle bound people on Muscle Beach, and racquetball people on the racquetball courts. The boardwalk was lined with concessions, but they pretty much just sold beach paraphernalia, food, refreshments and health foods like Tiger Shakes. We had windows looking out over the ocean all the way across the front side of the flat, which was the view from the large 40 x 15 foot front room.

The 'boardwalk' in front of our place was actually asphalt. Between the asphalt and the beach was lawn. One night, during a full eclipse of the moon we camped out on the lawn so we could see it. It always surprises the mind when a major aspect of the physical universe like the moon does something unusual. It usually just sits up there like a silver dollar in the sky. Suddenly as the earth's shadow moves across, the roundness like a ball is visible. It was like a mystic secret unveiling itself, suspending time and motion, while no one else in the whole world was paying attention, and then it started going back to its original form ever so slowly.

Time, space, and form are never still and yet, in the stillness, there is a magical presence that constantly reveals itself in the concept. These conceptions that seem so real to the senses and faculties of sight, feeling, hearing, touching, grasping, thinking, and loving are in a constant state of becoming and then not being. What wondrous thing lies in between? What is that? Why do I *have* such wonderful thoughts? Is there some majestic meaning beckoning in the silence, the "in" space beyond time? What real experience exists there, the source of definition for all of that which we call meaning? Is it so different from all relative association as to defy thought and the spoken word? Is it the sound of "one hand clapping?"

If everything is sound and light that intensifies and dissipates or comes and goes in multitudes of frequencies, then what about sound and light in the reality, from whence the definition of the ephemeral state we are experiencing comes? What experiences occur there? Surely there is a capability within our being to explore that, or why do we ask? So goes the mind of the truth seeker. Is the seeking caused by the seeker or that which is being sought? Isn't it interesting how sometimes questions that beg for answers say much, much, much more than that which can be conjured by the mind in the form of an answer? The moon finally went back to being a silver dollar in the sky and I lay there till practically dawn, unable to sleep because of the wonder of it.

Some of our beat friends from San Francisco had moved to Venice Beach. Paul Osborne (an actor) and his wife Carol came by. Paul had a very regal disposition (I thought he looked like Elvis Presley) with a completely different personality, more English in his demeanor. He always talked as if he was expressing poetic oratory. His very pretty wife, Carol, was an intellectual who seemed to know everything about everything.

Then there was the seriously quiet Cameron with long flaming red hair. "You know she's a witch," Mike confided in me one day. Apparently she had been involved with the famous Warlock (or so they say) Alister Crowley. Whatever she was or wasn't, whether any of it was true or not, or what it meant, was pretty insignificant to us. For the most part in my experience with 'wiccans', they were different, but no more than all of our other friends, and their occult status was always benign and they never tried to preach to us.

Then there was Big Black, the conga player. He was big and black and very much like Girard in Santa Barbara – a lot of fun. What a great spirit he manifested.

One day our piano player friend, Dutch, from the "Boom-Boom" in Santa Barbara, came and picked us up in an old Plymouth in very nice condition and took us to Newport Beach. When we got there, he dropped us off and Jean said "this is where we're going to live, boys, but first we have to find a rental." So we went from street to street looking for a rental.

Lee and I finally knocked on a door that was answered by an elderly couple. "We're looking for a 2 bedroom apartment for a family of five, we saw your sign – is yours still available?"

"Sure, where's your folks?"

"We'll go get them – see you in about five or ten minutes!" We brought Peter and Jean back and that was it. They invited us in, served us cookies and tea, shook hands on the deal, and the next day we moved in.

Newport beach was a major surfing town. The local youth were divided up into three basic groups; surfers, socies (so-shees), and hoedads. The surfers wore low-top sneakers or canvas deck shoes with levis, tee shirt, Pendelton shirt and/or corduroy sports coat, or blue windbreaker with light fleece lining, or Hawaiian shirt (that was really hip). The soshies dressed ivy league, and the hoedads adopted the cool, slightly bad, hoodlum look popularized on television by the "Fonz" on Happy Days, black leather jacket, blue jeans, and white shirt. I was a "hoedad" and quickly acquired the name "L.A." I still combed my hair like Elvis, so it was a pretty hard image to shake, even though I was attracted to the sea like some kind of amphibious creature that couldn't stay out of the ocean for too long. I loved to ride the waves with my body. I found out they had a name for it: Body Surfing. I thought "Wow, that almost makes me a surfer," except I think you were supposed to have a surfboard to ride to be called a surfer.

The fall had arrived, the miraculous Pittsburgh Pirates had beaten the Yanks in the World Series, but I had exchanged baseball for body surfing. Some of the surfers I knew from school had little trailers they hooked up to their bikes and carried their surfboards that way. Others just put the board under their arms and road their bike with one hand. They would build a fire because it was generally chilly and the water was cold. They would congregate near the pier where we lived.

So, I would come up out of the water and stand around the fire with them. "Hey L.A., nice jacket! Are you a surfer now?" I was chided. I had actually found a blue jacket like one of theirs in the bushes over by the Balboa yacht harbor and it fit perfectly. It was great for putting on when I got out of the water instead of drying off with a towel. I knew they were being friendly. I no longer combed my hair like Elvis, and my long blond hair was hanging all over my head like they wished their parents would let them grow theirs.

"Well, I'm just body surfing until I get a board and learn how to surf."

"Cool," one said, "the surf is really great here."

I usually body surfed farther north closer to home. It was better for board surfing close to the pier.

One day in December it was warm and sunny and I was out body surfing but the water had become very cold, in fact most of the surfers were wearing wet suits. I was in the water a long time and when I got out I couldn't stop shivering. I must have been on the verge of hypothermia. A very nice couple sitting out on their beach patio saw me standing in the sun nearby trying to get warm, but relentlessly shivering and they said "Come on over here and get wrapped in a blanket before you freeze to death!"

I wasn't going to argue, so I said "ssh-sure, th-th-thanks" and sat there looking at the beautiful blue ocean and the bright beige colored sand while they explained that they were marine biologists and they lived by the ocean to better study it.

"What do your parents do?" "My father's a painter and my mother is a poet" I replied.

"We'd like to meet them sometime" they said.

"Well they're hardly ever home, they're in L.A. most of the time, getting ready for a show on La

Cienega Boulevard, but next time I get a chance I'll try to bring them over."

Since the biologists were always home, their patio became a hangout for my brother Lee and our friends, which was cool because they seemed to enjoy having us around. Peter and Jean eventually met them and were very pleased that I had made such interesting friends. Around Christmas, we were all invited over to make Christmas cookies of all kinds and practice Christmas songs for caroling. It's so beautiful how people just sometimes come together and for a brief period become like a family.

Kennedy had just been elected President and it was like a page had been turned from one chapter in our life to another. Peter was having success with his painting and he was actually creating a presence in the art scene in Southern California, the center of which was La Cienega Blvd. in West Hollywood. Peter and Jean had been reading about Zen Buddhism (writings by Alan Watts, D.T. Suzuki, Huang Po and all things Zen, like Haiku, Bonsai, and Sumi Ink drawing) and the interesting thing was that instead of saying "that's what we want to be" they were saying "that's what we are, that's the life we've been living."

Peter and Jean visited Laguna Beach, which still is an art colony that had been started early in the 20th century. First, they found a tiny gallery on the South Coast Highway, which is what the Pacific Coast Highway is called south of Long Beach, and then they found a three-bedroom apartment (so Mike could have his own room) in a beautiful ravine just south of Calliope and Glenleyre. That weekend they came home and said, "We're moving to Laguna Beach."

23 Laguna Beach

Laguna has always been one of my favorite
places in the world, a world apart from Newport,
yet only fifteen miles south. Newport is pretty
much of a beach town without even the sand
dunes found farther north. Laguna is hilly with
ravines, cliffs and rock formations, and tidal
pools along the beach. Instead of one long beach.
it is naturally broken up into numerous beaches
and coves. The public and private landscapes
are covered with a myriad varieties of native and
exotic conifers, palms, Birds of Paradise, citrus,
flowering shrubs and ground covers, ornamentals
of almost any kind including Bougainvillea.
Each little beach and cove has a different kind of
surf break, including point breaks (where a wave
breaks off a peninsula-type point and works its
way across the beach), reef breaks (breaks caused
by off-shore reefs), and beach breaks (breaks
caused by the bottom as it proceeds from shallow
to deep from the beach). We called the surf spot
by the name of the street that went down to it
or the cliff above it. Agate Street was the beach I
usually went to after school. It was a good body
surfing spot, usually a beach break, but if swell

was big enough there was a rock formation point with an arch and tidal pools where the waves would start to break their way across the beach. A half mile north there was a much larger point with tidal pools and reefs that extended out that was called Brooks Street. This was where the biggest break was, especially if the swell was over ten feet, and breaking off the second or third reef out. Although Oak St., the next surfing spot down, had a reef even farther out called Ringers Reef. It was said to accommodate the biggest swells when everywhere else was un-ridable. Usually Oak Street waves broke closer in, off closer reefs. That eventually became my favorite spot because it was big, fast, and as it got closer to the beach it developed a critical curl. The next one down (there was also one in between that was quite good although I can't remember the name) was Thalia Street, which was a lot like Oak Street with less shape and not quite as interesting, but also a lot of fun. Next to that was St. Ann's, which I liked a lot because, as I mentioned in a previous chapter, it would close out causing you to ride it straight in and then as it approached the beach it would form a new break and you could turn your body like a surfboard and ride it on the shoulder just in front of the break all the way into the beach.

The next beach down was Main beach – as far
as I usually wandered, right in front of the small
downtown.   It was the largest and usually most
populated beach, with waves that pretty much
just came straight in and broke all at once. This
is what we called a body womping spot. That
meant riding the wave one of three ways: just
ride it straight in and hope you can survive the
crunch; go "over the falls" which meant taking
the lip of the break straight over, "kamikaze"
style then continuing the circle at the bottom
and coming up the other side; or take off as if it
had an angular break (my favorite) get a really
fast tubular but short ride, turn into the wave at
the bottom and come up the other side.

Laguna Zen

In one moment, O lonely pine
With your gnarled trunk
And crooked branches
The story of life untold
How gently green needles
Explode in clear lines
Piercing the space
Around the lighted windows of home.
Eucalyptus and pine ambrosia
Permeate the night

Japanese lanterns light up the inside
Where Peter is using bold strokes
Of blue, green, red, black, and yellow
To create a living passion,
Of form, texture, and dimension,
Defined by colors
Opaque and translucent,
And shapes and lines that continue to live,
After the strokes are made,
While Coltrane, Miles, Evans, Kelly,
Chambers, Philly Joe, Cobb,
Cannonball, Monk, and Shankar
Fill the air.
Jean looks up, You're just in time,
Dinner is ready."
The waves still pound
And massage the rocks and sand
Under the moon, All at once.

I always walked to school with Todd and Kim,
two boys my age that lived across the ravine from
us. As we walked along, we were joined by a very
pretty brown-haired, blue-eyed girl. "Hi Todd, hi
Kim, who's this?"

"Hi Robin, this is Pat; Pat this is Robin."

"Pleased to meet you, Robin!" Indeed I was.
Robin had unforgettable eyes, and a real sense of
enjoyment about her.

"Do you surf?" she asked.

"No," I replied, " haven't learned yet, but I'm a very good swimmer and I love body surfing."

"I'd be glad to teach you," she offered. "My mother is the World Women's Champion, Marge Calhoun, and my sister Candy is the girl's teen-age World Champion."

"Wow!" that would be great! But first I have to get a surfboard,"

"Meanwhile you'll have to come and hang out with us at Oak Street," Robin invited.

"It's a date," I replied.

"I'll be there Saturday" she said.

"Then I will too."

For a while, she was my first real girlfriend. She met Peter and Jean and we talked about art, surfing, and boats. Her big sister was an artist and she was fascinated with the fact that Peter was an artist and actually had paintings in progress in the living room. However, her mother was a professional surfer, so they traveled and I didn't see much of her after a couple of weeks.

Every day after school, I would go down to the beach and body surf. In wood shop at school, I built a skim board: you run and throw it down on one-half inch of receding water on the beach after a wave and skim along until you hit the water. When I got tired of that, I would go out and catch some waves.

Another thing that happened at school was scuba lessons. At first Agate Street was a very lonely beach, but every once in a while I would see Doosenbury, the classical beach bum. Actually that was just his facade. He was a seasoned body surfer and I loved to hear his stories about the swells. His personality was almost exactly like Jeff Bridges, a man of few words, but always interesting.

One night we went to see the Academy Awards on TV with our friends, Alan and Jane Rosen, another Laguna Beach artist and his wife. They were communists. They never talked about it and didn't do anything about it, but there you are. I really liked them and we always enjoyed their company. They had a really neat gadget that turned off the sound of the TV commercials when they came on.

I was now fourteen and having a lot of fun playing baseball. As summer approached, I even qualified for a Babe Ruth League team. My uniform was hanging in the closet. But Peter's paintings were selling and he had a plan. "Let's live in Puerto Vallarta."

I was going to miss Laguna Beach. Coming in after sunset to find Peter painting, Jean cooking and jazz playing ("Sketches of Spain" or "Monk & Trane", or "Kind of Blue" by Miles Davis, or perhaps Ravi Shankar or Trane's "Giant Steps"), the parties, the make-out sessions, the friends and the surf. But going to Mexico actually trumped all that. Next to the surf, and girls, the hottest topic on the beach was a surfing safari to Mexico! So, with our bags on our backs and a ride to Tijuana with some friends, we were on our way.

24 Adios California, Hola Mexico

When we got to Tijuana, we got our bus tickets for the first leg of our trip. Peter was in the men's room and put his wallet on the top of the stall momentarily, then started out without it, but when he went back in to get it, it was gone. At least Jean had some money. One thing for sure there was no going back. We never went back. Sometimes after a number of years, we returned. We returned—to New York, Sarasota, Mexico City, San Francisco, Madeira Beach—after we left some other place, but we never started out and then turned back.

Every trip had a life of its own. The trip to Vallarta would have to be as cheap as possible, short of hitchhiking, until we got to the tropics. Then we hitchhiked. We had to make what money was left last until more money came from the Plummer Gallery.

We got rides from farmers mostly and slept under the stars. As we headed south it became greener and cooler and the people seemed happier and more hospitable. Another adventure was under full swing. We bathed in deliciously cool and refreshing irrigation ditches.

South of Tepic, it started to rain heavily and a family invited us to stay with them. In the morning, we had a delicious breakfast of beans and tortillas and vegetable soup. Before we took off we helped plant corn in some rich humus soil, earth as dark as dark roast coffee, that still crumbled nicely in spite of the rain. You just made a small hole with one hand and put in three kernels of corn with the other. What a simple but beautiful life they had– simple handmade abodes, vegetable gardens, a nearby forest or jungle with mangos, papayas, bananas, coconuts, coffee and other paradisiacal flora and fauna.

To get to Vallarta in those days, you had to go by boat, private plane or on a jungle bus. These were crafted from a flat bed truck with very large twin tires and chains, because the roads were very bad and rocky. On the flatbed, were seats and an open-air canopy. South of Campostelo, it was 50 miles to Puerto Vallarta and no paved roads. It would be at least two years before Elizabeth Taylor, Richard Burton, Ava Gardner, and John Huston would make it famous with the movie, "The Night of the Iguana."

Because of rain, the roads were especially bad and we got stuck at least two times before we would get to our destination– Puerto Vallarta, three or four miles past the river that separates the States of Nayarit and Jalisco. The river was high and crossing would be difficult. We had to carry our bags over our heads so swimming was out of the question, and if the current swept us off our feet and we might lose our bags. Somehow we all made it across with our bags. Our actual destination was Yelapa, which was on the south side of the bay. We slept on the beach that night, then after breakfast we went to Playa de Los Muertos Beach on the south end of Vallarta. The trip would take an hour and a half by boat. Nowadays, the beach is broken up by jetties into little beaches in front of each hotel. Back then there were no hotels except the Oceano and the Rosarita and the beaches were open and free as far as you could see or imagine.

On the way to catch our boat, we stopped at the river mouth in the center of town. Although the surf was small, the local boys were riding the perfectly shaped waves on small wooden planks. Farther on down was the beach called, "Playa de Los Muertos," or Beach of the Dead, so named because there was a cemetery nearby. Interestingly, except for the whorehouse up on the hill on the other side of the river, this was (and still is) the partying side of town, called "La Zona Romantica," or the Romantic Zone.

At that time there was no pier, so you had to wade out to the boat, which meant getting through the shore break with our bags on our heads again. Once aboard, we were headed across the bay to Yelapa.

Because of the Zen Buddhist philosophy we had adopted, we were vegetarians. But being the vagabonds we were, eating fish was not out of the question, so when the skipper gave us fishing poles, we were eager to try our luck. Before long, I felt a bite and started reeling something in. Whatever it was, it was big, because it really put up a fight. About fifty feet off the stern, it jumped out of the water. It was a very beautiful mahi-mahi, about 3-4 feet long. A mahi-mahi is a rainbow colored fish much bigger than a trout. However, before we could land it, it got away. Though we had no more bites, before we got to Yelapa, we saw porpoises, whales and sea turtles.

As we pulled into the lagoon where Yelapa was located, it suddenly occurred to me that we were in paradise. There was a waterfall coming out of the mountainside just above the village of thatched roof dwellings (palapas). When we got off the boat, we asked where we might find Tom Newman. Eventually a delightfully nice

lady introduced herself as Peggy and said that
Tom and Brice (a friend of Tom Newman's) were
out of town right now but perhaps we could
find lodging with John Langley, who had a large
palapa at the river mouth. By the disembarkment
beach was a large palapa with a cement floor
with tables and chairs – a restaurant of sorts. It
was a good place for a respite until we made our
next move. Peter asked the person serving us if
they had horchata and was pleasantly surprised
when he said, "Si, Señor." Horchata (silent "h",
rhymes with piñata) is a drink made from rice
powder and water, sweetened and spiced with
vanilla and cinnamon, or just cinnamon.

So we sat there soaking in our paradisical
surroundings on a beautiful day in the month
of May, 1961, as we enjoyed our horchatas.
Next, we took a walk on a dirt path that wound
around through the slightly hilly jungle, along
the rocky shore, for about a half mile. We came
to a compound with a very large palapa and two
small ones nearby, on about 2 acres that had
been cleared out of the jungle. A man with long
curly red hair and a beard came walking out to
greet us with nothing on except a sarong (a band
of cloth of colorful design in this case) around
his waist. A manly skirt in a Tahitian sort of
way. "Hi, my name's John Langley. Welcome to

Yelapa!" he exclaimed, with a radiant smile on his golden-earringed face.

As the adults became acquainted, we boys decided to look for the bottom of that waterfall. In about twenty minutes, we were looking up from a sandy, pebbly, pool of water (about the size of your average 500 square foot pool) at this beautiful waterfall gushing from a small river about 200-300 feet up, uninterrupted for the most part, until it hit the pool below. In the coming days and weeks, we would return there almost daily.

The only things we brought for the kitchen were a large bowl-shaped frying pan called a "wok", a pot to cook rice or beans in, five spoons, chopsticks, five bowls, five cups, and a knife to cut vegetables. We also had an espresso pot that you flipped over when the water boiled that we had had since early Florida days.

One day, I offered to go across the lagoon to the only store in town and get some green coffee beans, which we would roast in the wok. On the beach was a small dugout boat that we were allowed to use. It was called a "kayuko." It had a paddle and I always enjoyed paddling over to town and back. On the way back, it had become stormy and the wind was blowing the kayuko out to sea. Even when I paddled harder it was still blowing me out. Then I realized I would have to paddle as hard as I could until I got to the other side. Paddling harder and faster, realizing my life depended on it and using every ounce of strength I had, I had an orgasm. When I finally got to the other side I realized the coffee beans had spilled all over the bottom of the kayuko. I salvaged as many as I could and they took longer to roast because they were wet, but they made good coffee with a flavor only I could fully appreciate.

I made friends with a beautiful soul named Domingo, who was three or four years older than me. He made life interesting in Yelapa. He showed me a lemon tree so we had an abundant supply of lemonade, and how to catch crawfish in the river, and how to transplant tomato seedlings that volunteered from behind the restaurant, and how to sing "Cielito Lindo."

John Langley had a short-wave radio. We listened to the launch of a satellite and later saw it crossing the sky. Often, he would take out his guitar and sing folk songs, Burl Ives style. Years before, he had been a concert violinist and he shot off his index finger to collect the insurance. One night he invited us over for a dinner of raw fish fixed the way he learned in Tahiti, marinated in juice rendered from grating fresh coconut on

a special grating device he had brought from
Tahiti. In fact, the reason he had settled in Yelapa
was because it was so much like Tahiti.

On Saturday night, there was a dance at the
restaurant with the big cement floor. In between
dancing, we were drinking shots of raicilla,
bootleg tequila that was 180 proof (so they said).
Being all of fourteen, I was not an experienced
drinker. Peter and Jean were very light drinkers,
just the occasional glass of wine. We would go
for months with no alcohol in the house at all.
I soon passed out, laying my head on the table,
and then in short order puked, which woke me
up. I was helped to a nearby palapa where I slept
it off. We were not invited back.

Right behind our palapa, there was a mother
and daughter living together. Jean would make
tortillas with them, showing them how it was
done in the Yucatan, and they showed Jean how
they did it. The daughter's name was Pilar and
the mother's name was Hirlaria. One day, I was
paddling in the lagoon and a very large white
shark, almost as big as the kayuko, came up close
to the surface turning sideways up, probably to
survey the part of what he could see under water
that was above water. We both got a good look
at each other. "That guy could flip the kayuko
and have me for lunch," I thought, "and I'm

not sticking around to see if he figures it out." I quickly paddled to shore. When I told some of the locals they said "Yeah, there's lots of sharks out there, but there's also a lot of fish for them to eat. They never attack anybody. Nevertheless, I stopped swimming in the lagoon.

Weeks went by and there was still no word from the Plummer gallery. Brice finally showed up and said Tom wouldn't be coming for awhile. The jungle is an amazing thing. When we first arrived it was forbiddingly thick. There was an impenetrable energy about it. There was a constant loud noise of insects that seemed to say, "Stay Out!" Domingo also told me about "El Tigre." Evidently, jaguars roamed about in the jungle.

The village, however, always seemed very benign. There was the occasional iguana, a scary looking anachronism from the reptilian age that were three to four feet long, but it was a vegetarian that was very wary of humans because it was considered a delicacy that tasted like chicken. There was possibility of displeasure that might be visited upon anyone who dared to remove a banana from the perennial stalk that hung in John Langley's palapa, until they had fully ripened with brown spots and all, and there were boisterous tropical birds like parrots, that used Yelapa for a breeding ground, that might startle a person.

We finally got word from the Plummer Gallery. It had burned down and the paintings were uninsured! So there we were, more than a thousand miles from an income source, and pretty much broke. Somehow Peter and Jean worked out passage back to Vallarta and there was a little palapa on the beach we could rent for 30 pesos a month, which was 8 cents a day. We got off the boat and walked almost to Nayarit, or so it seemed.

Vallarta was much smaller then and we were just beyond the first river mouth going north along the beach and there it was– a very small A-frame palapa with the river on one side and the bay on the other. At the entrance, which was always open (no door), was an open fireplace– just a ring of stones in the sand, but perfect for cooking with our wok.

However, at that point we were mostly concerned about having something to put *in* the wok. Jean and Peter went into town to sell a pair of Jean's high heels. At that time, money was scarce in Puerto Vallarta, so they figured their best market was the whorehouse on the hill above town. They managed to get enough pesos to feed us for a few days, and then it was a blouse or a dress, and so forth, until Jean had very little left to wear.

We spent our days exploring Vallarta, swimming, and making friends. In a big field along the river, I found a bunch of young guys, most of them a little older than me, playing baseball. Before we left Laguna Beach, as I said, I was having a good baseball year, and I figured if I got a chance to bat, I'd put one in the river. They were good sports and invited me to join their game. However, their pitching was better than I thought and in my two at bats I struck out and popped up. But they were great guys and it was a lot of fun.

The biggest and best player was very friendly and hospitable and asked me if I wanted to join them for a swim. "Sure," I said, so he took us to a swimming hole on the river where we could dive from some rocks. We swam across and I saw them throwing rocks up into a very tall tree. It was a mango tree and the only mangoes that would fall were the ripe ones.

The next night we walked into town to see what the nightlife was like. We walked along the "Malaccan," which was a wide sidewalk along the cobblestone street that ran along the oceanfront, and along the sidewalk was a seawall that you could sit on like a bench. At sunset people would walk and socialize there as well as in the plaza in the center of town. In those days there were homes on the strip of land where the river forked into two rivers. As we were crossing through, I noticed that people were visiting each other and enjoying each other's food. I saw my baseball friend and he said, "Hola Patricio! Come and meet my people! Try some of this – try some of that," corn, beans, vegetables, tortillas and more, which I enjoyed greatly as I was always hungry.

One day Peter and Jean came home with some old friends from San Francisco, George Connolly and Phyllis Dillon. They had just flown in and were staying at *The Rosarita*. That night we all sat around the fire telling old stories. The next day I saw George on the beach sitting on a seawall with the fishermen bringing in their catch.

"This is a beautiful scene here, do you like it?" asked George.

"It's been a great summer so far, it's a different life here," I answered.

"I wish I could speak Spanish, it makes you feel out of place when you can't speak the language."

"Well, stick around long enough and you'll learn."

"Yeah," he said, "I suppose. It's a nice change coming to paradise, but I miss the city, miss my pad, my haunts, my restaurants, but mostly my people."

"Huh!" I said, "I guess we've always moved around so wherever we go it ends up being my people—there, here, wherever."

"Well, you might as well enjoy it, you obviously won't be here forever."

"That's probably right." My mind had moved on to planning my day.

"I think I'll go for a swim by the river mouth, and maybe play some baseball. I guess we're all meeting at Tom McGhee's later, see you then."

"Later, man." As I walked along the beach in front of the Malaccan, the walk above the beach and behind the seawall, I saw my brother Mike. He was now 16 and a very attractive young man, walking along with a beautiful lady about 3 or 4 years his senior, hand in hand. I yelled, "Hey, Mike!"

"Hi, Pat!" He hadn't been sleeping in the palapa lately and now I knew why. He had become friends with a Don Juan type beach boy at the palapa restaurant at Playa de Los Muertos, who liked to tell stories of his romantic escapades, and how as a result he bought a home for his mother and one for himself.

Tom McGhee lived over near Pancho Lepe's and when I got there, everybody was excited about something. "I know you boys have already started drinking, which is really stupid, so today we're going to introduce you to something different that is non-addictive, and won't destroy your organs or your general health, unlike alcohol or hard drugs which will," sermonized Jean. "Actually, much like peyote, (which they grew and ate in Florida) we consider this as a sacrament for elevating the consciousness," Jean continued. "The idea is that we can elevate our consciousness without anything. The high is not in the pot, it's already inside you waiting to be unlocked." With that the pipe was lit and passed around.

George always liked Puerto Vallarta and being with us, but for reasons already mentioned, he decided to go back to San Francisco. Phyllis, however, stayed and moved in with us. That night someone else snuck into the palapa and left before dawn. In the morning Phyllis announced, "I've got to wash my sheets. Tom McGhee came and slept with me last night!" Later on we saw Tom and asked him if he had been there in the middle of the night.

"No, I was home all night." I guess we'll never know who it was. Phyllis went back to San Francisco shortly thereafter.

One day, I noticed an American couple in the store near our palapa asking directions to Pancho

Lepe's house. Pancho Lepe was a special friend to some of the local Americans and was helpful in finding a place for people to rent.

"Hi, can I help? I speak Spanish," I offered.

"Please do. My name's Jerry and this is Judy. We're trying to find some friends that are staying in the area and we were told to contact Pancho Lepe," Jerry said with an infectious smile, obviously happy about his luck in finding a Spanish speaking American.

"I can help you there. Pancho Lepe is in a neighborhood over on the other side of Vallarta behind Playa de los Muertos. If you go to the big palapa restaurant on the beach, they'll tell you how to get there. Somebody will speak English there."

"Thanks a lot, maybe we'll see you around."

"Yeah, that'd be great." Off they went on the horses they rode in on. Evidently they had bought horses in Tepic because they were told it was the best way to get to Vallarta.

Like us, they had arrived in Vallarta broke, so they sold one of the horses after they talked to Pancho Lepe. They were a very likeable couple except they were constantly fighting. They had, unbeknownst to me, come down with Bob Burton, a friend of ours from Venice Beach. He looked like Omar Sharif with a beard, she looked like Jane Fonda (in their early twenties.) Later that afternoon, I saw three people and a horse silhouetted by the setting sun coming up the beach toward our palapa. As they got closer I thought, "That looks like Jerry and Judy, and I wonder who that short roundish, Zen monk-looking fellow is with them?" – think a short Toshiro Mifune from Rashomon, but more round. "Why, that's Bob Burton!" Except Bob Burton had always worn a navy blue business suit with white shirt and black tie. He was truly a transformed man.

One day I made friends with a guy from Ann Arbor, Michigan. His name was John and he invited me to join him for ice cream at an ice cream shop off the Plaza. We were listening to the jukebox, and I asked him, "So, what's new in the States?"

"Well, there's a new song called 'Stay' he replied.

"Cool," (maybe I said 'bitchen'), "let's see if it's on the jukebox," I suggested. We sauntered over to the jukebox which was playing "Mother-in-Law."

"There it is!" John announced. "I'll play it so you can check it out." Next thing you know we were listening to the latest #1 in the States in '61, "Stay!.. just a little bit longer ... ."

"So what's it like in Ann Arbor? I don't suppose there's any surf on Lake Michigan?"

"No, not really, sometimes when it gets stormy we get small waves."

"The surf's not that great here either, we're not really on the Pacific and by the time waves get in here, there's not much to 'em. I'm hoping for a Pacific storm to send some big ones in."

"Do you surf?" Asked John.

"Nah, I've never had a board, but I like to body surf."

John's father was a professor at Michigan State and his obviously well to do family was staying in one of those homes along the beach that we would pass on the way out to our palapa. When we came to John's we sat in the cabana out in front and shortly a waiter came over and asked if we would like anything. "Two cokes please," ordered John. As we sat there looking at the sunlight sparkling like diamonds on the deep blue colored ocean, John asked, "Have you ever been to a whorehouse, Pat?"

"No, I never have, but I can tell you they were a major topic of conversation among the surfers on the beach in Laguna, and seemed like no surfing safari story was complete without mentioning a night in a whorehouse," I replied, not bothering to mention that I was a virgin.

"I hear they have one here in Vallarta," John commented.

"I know they do, my mom's been selling the whores items from her wardrobe."

"You wanna go?"

"I haven't got that kind of money," I said.

"I'll pay for the both of us," offered John.

"Well, I would never forgive myself if I turned down that offer."

"It's set then, we'll meet here at 8:00 and Jorge, our guide, will take us up." Later on we were led to a house across the street from the whorehouse, which had a red light over the door. We were invited in and sat on a large bed, and I was thinking, "Is this where we do it?"

After waiting about a half hour we were taken across the street to a large hotel-type building built around a courtyard with tables to sit at and drink raicilla with the girls we would sleep with. It was a beautiful summer night and they had a mariachi band wandering around playing and singing.

Finally somebody said, "Pat, you can take her up to the room whenever you want."

"Well what are we waiting for?" I said. So we got up and I followed her up to the room where we took our clothes off and I did what I always thought I would do, and as soon as things got wet she pushed me off and I asked "Ya?" (is that it?) and she said "Ya." "That was weird," I thought, "oh well it was fun and it was free."

The next day we went horseback riding and John asked, "How was it?"

"It was great!" I said.

"That's not what she said, according to Jorge," corrected John.

"Well, *I* thought it was great, I don't know what to tell you except, thanks."

As people would come and go I began to feel like a local. Tom McGhee showed me down south around the bend from Playa de los Muertos where there were little coves with rocks that had large Pacific oysters underneath. We would bring a knife and some lemons and break 'em off, break 'em open and eat 'em right there on the beach and the rocks.

Just as I had hoped, a storm came and with it big waves. After the storm, I walked a couple miles north to a very large river mouth where very large waves, ten-plus feet high, were peaking and pluming with an off shore breeze. They were beautiful to watch, but I knew I couldn't body surf them without fins. Without fins a large wave like that eats you up before you can start riding it.

Back at the palapa everyone was getting up and having pancakes. I tried to tell them about the waves but no one was listening. Later on, I found that the best body surfing waves, without fins, were at Playa de los Muertos. Mike, Lee and Bob Burton, John and I had a great time with those waves all day. And so went the summer. A fourteen year old's dream summer.

It was almost September and Bob Burton had gotten some money to go home and attend his mother's funeral. We sold him an antique golden Buddha from Thailand for $80.00, which was enough to get us to the border.

Half way to Matamoros (we were going back to Miami, Florida this time) my right foot was itching. When I took my shoe off to scratch it, it rapidly started to swell and within a half hour it was almost like a football. It was an interior bacterial infection and by the time we got to Corpus Christi I had to be hospitalized for a week while I got antibiotic treatments. Somehow, Peter and Jean had managed to procure a week's lodging nearby, but being totally broke we had to hitchhike from Corpus Christi, Texas, to Miami.

25 Florida or Bust(ed)

So there we were lined up on the highway, three boys 12, 14 and 16, and mom and dad, with our bags at our feet – Miami here we come! Traveling salesmen, a traveling minister, drunken partiers sometimes driving 80-90 miles per hour (scary), people hoping we had money for gas, and others from all walks of life. By the next day in the morning we were hitchhiking through Louisiana. Coffee was 5 or 10 cents a cup so we drank coffee with cream. "You know I'm drinking coffee with cream now for the nutrition," Peter said.

One night in Pensacola at 3 or 4 in the morning, we were half hitch hiking, half lying all over our bags when a cop pulled over to ask questions. "What are you doing here with your kids like this?"

"We're trying to get to Miami."

"Well this just isn't legal keeping your kids out this late loitering in the streets."

"We're doing the best we can officer, there's work for me in Miami."

"I'm sorry, I'm going to have to haul you all down to the precinct." Jean had a 16-ounce mayonnaise jar full of marijuana, which would have amounted to felony possession. So when we got to the police station she rolled it under the squad car, a move unnoticed by even me, so when we were inside and they were searching our bags, we were all worried about that. They never found it, but we still ended up in jail for the weekend. The jail was seriously dilapidated with rust, chipping paint, and filth. It was beyond my comprehension that they could treat children this way, let alone adults.

In court on Monday the Judge told the cop, "What are you doing bothering these people? I want you to take them outside the city limits and drop them off." Then we got a ride with an ice cream truck that let us off in front of a watermelon patch with watermelons that were growing wild. Delicious! A lot better than jail food.

Going through a town south of Pensacola, we got into a car and the driver was playing Ray Charles' "Hit the Road Jack," with which we could really identify. The next day we got a ride with an itinerant farmer family hoping we had gas money because they were broke too. They would coast down one hill and drive up the other side. "We're going to let you off here at this public beach where there's a restroom and hopefully we can find someone to help with the gas up ahead."

The sunset, the stars came out. We decided to get some sleep on the beach and a fresh start in the morning. Around nine or ten that morning, a lady in a big fancy car drove up and gave Jean a check for $100.00. "Never give up on humanity," she said as she drove off. Now we had enough money to take the bus to Miami.

When we got to Miami in late September, Peter was able to get work doing antique restoration and we were able to live in the catamaran of our old friends from Sarasota, Tuni and Ralph. Lee went to a junior high school nearby, and Mike and I went to Miami Jackson High School, about a mile away. I was a freshman. School had already started by two or three weeks. I got a job selling papers on a busy street so I was making a little money to help out with my own small expenses. Every once in a while, I would get a tip though I didn't really expect it. One day a waitress bought the paper and said, "I'm sorry honey, but nobody's tipping me either." I could tell some people really depended on tips. When Jean waitressed, she didn't say much unless she got a lot of good tips, so I never thought about what it felt like to work and get no tips.

Peter and Jean's friend, the architect Bill Rupp, who made the cover of *Look* magazine as one of America's 100 unsung heroes, was building a new home for himself and his wife and daughter. He wanted Peter to install teakwood cabinets throughout the house.

Our friends, the Strong's, had a second floor apartment across from their house that we used, so it was back to Sarasota and new schools. A friend of Dean Arnold's came down to get us because he had a station wagon. (You can imagine the conversation that probably took place.)

"Can you go down to Miami and move the Krohns up here to Sarasota?"

"Who are the Krohns?"

"A family of five – Mom, Dad and three teenage boys."

"Yeah, me and what Mayflower truck?"

"They don't have much, your station wagon ought to do the trick."

Of course when he arrived, I'm sure he was pleasantly surprised to see five people with five bags, which we threw in the back. We comfortably fit into the available seats. The Strong's had provided a large three bedroom apartment with a fireplace and a large grapefruit tree at the front door.

Lee and I went to Sarasota Jr. High (unlike
Miami, the ninth grade was included in junior
high) and Mike went to Sarasota High School.
They still had the Friday night dances at the
Youth center. For some reason, it wasn't as
exciting anymore. Everybody was my age. When
I tried out for the Babe Ruth League, I seemed
to do well in the field, but when I came to bat I
was so anxious that, even though I was making
good contact with the ball, I pulled everything
just foul of the third base line. But they couldn't
get me to strike out. Then, they brought in their
ace, but I kept doing the same thing. Finally,
they gave up and said, "Next!" I actually made
the team.

Peter and Jean had a young black friend that
came by once in a while, which was really cool
because the Jim Crow environment was very
strong at that time. In a world of conservatives
with little or no mixing of the races for the
most part, we were the progressives, not just
the liberals. I mean, in my mind, how could
you be a patriot, a lover of this country and its
constitutional freedoms and not be a liberal? And
to be progressive, that was a step farther. Besides
that, any prejudice or Jim Crow mentality was
something we abhorred. Those predispositions
and attitudes disgusted us. At any rate, Jim, our

black friend, was a schoolteacher, a jazz lover, and drove a really hot Corvair Monza Spider.

I remember he brought over Horace Silver's new release "Doin' the Thing." My favorite song was "Filthy McNasty," which was a totally outrageous abrogation of the current societal mores, even beyond the double entendre R&B records of the time. But the beauty of it was, that was just a name for some really fine music that made me feel, as Mr. Silver would say, "Like poppin' your finger, clappin' your hands, shakin' your hips, or shakin' whatever else you want to shake." The sounds were clear and strong and beautiful, the rhythm was exciting, and the riffs were clever, interesting and poetic. Yeah, we loved jazz in our house. For our part, (we had to leave Miles, and Monk, Shankar and Trane, and Gil Evans in Laguna Beach – they wouldn't fit in our bags, not to mention the record player) we had Mingus "Blues and Roots," Lambert Hendricks and Ross "the Hottest New Group on the Scene" (or something like that) and Billie Holiday. We never stayed in one place long enough to get a really extensive collection going, but what we had we listened to over and over. Our friend Jim had a special kind of spirit about him that was really beautiful, and we just enjoyed hanging out with someone like that. Ray

Draper, Lena Horne's son, Ted, and my wife's cousin Charles, and his wife Cindy, are also like that. It's not that so many other people aren't wonderful to be around and share time and communicate with, some people just have the gift to make you feel special just being in their presence, and to some degree maybe this is a subjective perception, but one I feel is shared by many others. If you have a friend like that, you are lucky indeed.

Some of the other records we heard over the years that I might not have mentioned included, a Katherine Dunham record recorded on site in places like Haiti, Cuba, Trinidad, West Indies and the like. Real tribal stuff with drums and other instruments, chanting, singing, Tororo – Haiti's greatest drummer – recorded in prison; Bunny Berrigan, "Inside Sauter and Finegan" (the two composers and arrangers) with Mundell Lowe (and an incredible rendition of "Old Folks"), New York 18 with Moondog and Serendipitous Street recordings, Yma Sumac, Gerry Mulligan and Chet Baker and other West Coast artists, and Harry Belafonte. These are some that come to mind.

One night, Mike and I went to a dance at the Armory where there was a real live band. Curtis Lee was supposed to be there but didn't show.

Now that Mike was in High School, he was
too old for the Youth Center by two years (this
was even my last year) so here he was, taking
me to his turf. And guess who was there – Jean
Williams. "Show Pat how we dance now," said
Mike. It was a slow dance and whereas Jean used
to bend over to dance with me before, now I was
taller than she was. The next thing I knew she
was grinding her pelvis against mine. I felt an
incredible sexual sensation, and I thought this
is all right! After the dance, Mike said, "Don't
get any ideas, she has a boy friend that you don't
want to mess with, and neither do I."

I came home one day to find – Bob Burton!
In Vallarta Bob had become like a brother. It was
so good to see him again. I haven't really said
much about him, but I haven't really said much
about my brothers either. That's because when
we were together we were like one, so when I
talk about things that happened they were either
with me or I was with them. It was like being
with myself. I took them for granted. I didn't
analyze them or take notes. We were together or
we weren't. Naturally, the three of us being two
years apart had different friends and interests,
so obviously we all have our own story that
intersected, fused or occurred side by side. They
were both charismatic and natural leaders and we

were all very independent and adventurous. So, this is all very subjective. Even when I'm trying to be objective, I can only talk about us from one perspective – mine.

Bob grew up in Cleveland, had a wild and crazy adolescence, where the students had sex on the school cafeteria tables, and then he went on to college because his parents expected him to be a doctor. He was well on his way, because he was very intelligent and capable, but he became involved in professional race car driving. He quit that because he enjoyed living. When we first met him, he was wearing a business suit and mentioned something about being in sales. At this point, he had decided he really wanted to be a Zen Buddhist Monk, and he thought Peter was a good example of that, so he liked being with us. However, if he spent too much time with Peter, Jean would become jealous so he spent more time with us, which is how he became like a big brother. He would share his thoughts like "I really think true enlightenment is the epitome of what I want in life, which means no desires because desires get in the way, self gratification gets in the way – so that means no sex – not even masturbation." I thought that sounded interesting but I wanted to have my cake (Zen philosophy) and to eat it too (somehow not giving up *all* desire).

The adults, including Bill Rupp and his wife Gwen, decided it was time to take peyote, so Bob Burton ordered some from the Native American Indian Church, who were only too eager to share their 'enlightenment' with the world. On peyote night, we all went over to the Rupp's new house for a night of music, conversation and hors d'oeuvres. I don't remember much, but I must have had a contact high because I was still awake at dawn. We were listening to Bach as the sun was rising. The light came in on the large wall-sized panes of glass, partially covered by long beautiful curtains, from the east side of the living room where we were sitting fully experiencing the miraculous birth of a new day. Maybe it was a heightened moment only because we stilled the mind adequately, and long enough, to experience the true *being* of our consciousness instead of just doing. Perhaps it was the initial stages of metaphysical doing or the existential experience of the American Indian spiritual consciousness that infiltrated the moment. Whatever it was, it was profound. Since I hadn't ever eaten any peyote, it was the first time I was aware of a higher consciousness within, and that substances like cannabis, peyote and sacred mushrooms were ultimately unnecessary in the pursuit and discovery of that.

One night, back when we were in Laguna Beach, we had talked about the possibility of atomic warfare and the book, "On the Beach," (which had also been made into a movie) was on everyone's mind. People were building bomb shelters, which in our case was unrealistic, so Peter had another idea. "My solution is to build a great big white bird. A 60-foot trimaran that could sail anywhere at speeds up to 40 knots (almost 50 mph) with a good short wave radio. We could avoid wars and radioactive clouds." According to studies and research done for the book, "On the Beach," the safest place from radioactive fallout would be Baja California, so it was decided the best place to build it would be California – our next destination.

By now we had moved out to the airport where Peter had a sail maker friend (probably the one who had made the sales for the Simplicity), Laddy Sadler, who had a space where Peter and Jean and now Bob Burton could perform boat repairs. There were also very austere living quarters and a shower with no hot water, and believe me, Sarasota can be cold in February. But we had a new plan. Peter had a large box of tools and a significant amount of building materials he had been acquiring for the trimaran. Unlike

Peter and Jean, Bob Burton had a driver's license and could be hired for a drive-away car (a car transport system which gave you transportation and the car owner a means of transporting their car). We would hook the trailer to a drive-away and Bob would drive us to California.

Mike, who was seventeen, decided he would have no part of this trip. He had a restaurant job and his friends, and he simply wanted to stay. Here we were, moving all the way across the country and Mike was staying in Sarasota. It was very difficult to imagine that now instead of five, we would be four. Of course, Bob Burton would now make us five again in a way, because we all liked Bob. He was a big help and a good friend.

26 On the Road Again

The drive-away turned out to be a very new Chevy that we would drive to St. Louis where we would get another to Los Angeles or San Francisco. When we got to St. Louis, we stopped for breakfast before we delivered the car, and the lady that owned the car drove by and saw the trailer hooked up to her brand new car. She flipped out. "That's my car! Look what they've done to it." Truth is they were already starting to make bumpers more flimsy and it was a little worse for the wear. In any case she took her car and we parked the trailer and waited there while Bob went to get another car. We never had a problem like that before. Just five bags. Things were changing for the Krohns. Pretty soon Bob came back with a fairly late model Pontiac Bonneville station wagon. This one had a much sturdier bumper. Next thing you know we were headed west on Route 66, which no longer exists, for the most part, like it was then. Unlike the super freeways you travel on now, it was a highway that generally became Main St. USA as it passed through each town.

"Hey Bob," I said, "This car's got an FM radio." Back in those days most cars just had AM radios.

"Cool, see if you can find a jazz station," he requested.

I actually found a DJ saying, "I've got a special treat for you tonight. I'm going to play two solid hours of Coleman Hawkins, the father of the modern tenor saxophone." For the next two hours, the sounds of the heart of Jazz carved their way through the night as only the "Hawk" could do, with the sound of the sax, song after song.

The next day we were driving through Flagstaff, Arizona, and I saw patches of snow for the first time, then we crossed the desert and soon we were up in the mountains between Palm Springs and San Bernadino. When we got to L.A. we were broke, so we sold the contents of the trailer and continued up the California coast to San Francisco. In Big Sur, we stopped to visit a friend. As they passed around their sweet smelling sacrament a spell was cast. It was as if we all understood something very beautiful was silently and subtly weaving its magic through the microcosmic fibers and ethereally fused spaces of our beings and in between the unknown elements of the moment. I sensed all this, yet without partaking of that substance, demonstrating it was already there within.

In the morning, as we wound our way along the mountainous coast, Mother Nature put on an incredible show of light and colors of green forest, blue sea, and sunrise shades of rose colors and blue sky, softly accented by fading clouds, mist and occasional sights of breaking waves on the rocky coast, and sea otters, seals, seagulls and blue jays. We stopped to walk among the majestic redwoods, shafts of light penetrating hundreds of feet to the forest floor, an intoxicating mixture of fragrances from trees, including bay laurel, shrubs and the earth's humus rich with life.

We were still towing the trailer, and if you've ever gone through Big Sur on Highway 1, you know that your brakes get hot even without the extra weight, so we stopped occasionally to let them cool and enjoy being still in paradise. We then dropped down into Carmel and took the 17-mile drive to Pacific Grove and Monterey, enjoying the timeless characteristics of nature that abound along there – the cypresses, the vivid blues of the ocean accentuated sometimes dynamically as the big white waves crashed on the rocky shore; colorful wharves of Steinbeck fame; on up to Santa Cruz and its beautiful cliffs.

Then came Half Moon Bay, a sleepy fishing town with a beautiful light house, and finally we drove into San Francisco on the Western Pacific side, through Golden Gate Park environs and the Marina and Presidio, on into North Beach, much the same as always, except we never had to find a place to park before.

Peter still had a rather large box of tools that would require two people to carry and a place to put it. Somehow we were able to contact Phyllis Dillon, who said we could stay at her pad. Once Bob got us settled in, I think he decided it was time to fly solo for a change. He was not to be seen again for some time further down the road, both actually and figuratively.

Phyllis had a very nice San Francisco apartment with the Victorian facade and curved window alcove off the living room. There was a brewery nearby that always gave the neighborhood a rich malty fragrance, interrupted only by the coffee smells of Italian coffee houses and Italian fresh bread just out of the oven. It was on Greenwich near Grant, just where you wanted to be in North Beach. The jazz FM radio was playing a lot of Woody Herman and Miles with Gil Evans, as well as everybody else. Phyllis had a record player and the three records I remember were of Charlie

Parker, Art Pepper and a Japanese Koto album. What a treat!

At school, I was in the final months of ninth grade as it was now April of '62. The ethnicity was a fairly even balance of Italian, Chinese, African-American, and others. I would get there early to play softball. There was also a new Italian kid named Marcello, who really looked sharp in a blond suit and tie with a white shirt and a complexion that matched. He was pretty much ignored by everyone because he couldn't speak English. I told him I could speak Spanish and it was amazing that we could communicate at all, but it was a lot better than trying to speak English. I never realized how different Italian was from Spanish, but by focusing on the similarities we managed, and of course that helped a little with creating a bridge to English. But I was more interested in girls, baseball, and dancing.

The dancing rage was the "mashed potatoes," which meant we were two dances separated from Rock and Roll, where partners held hands, a style that would never return universally to the way it was. However, the "mashed potatoes" we were doing at Francisco Jr. High School was much sexier and rhythmically more interesting than what was being done on American Bandstand. Instead of Charleston-looking foot movements, which were more the norm, we put our feet down on the ball and twisted not only at the ankle but with that whole side of the body, with the joints at odd angles to the rest of the body, and then did the same thing but different starting with the other foot, creating an improvisation of dance patterns that was both wild and sexy. The progenitors of this style were from the black contingency among us. Except they didn't refer to themselves as "black." This came to my attention when my Irish girlfriend and I were making out in a dark hallway under her apartment and next to us, making out, were a Chinese girlfriend and her black boyfriend. After the girls left he said, "You can't tell anybody about this because I'm a blood and we'd both get in a lot of trouble from everybody."

"You're a what?" I asked.

"I'm a blood."

"What does that mean?"

"It means I'm black." That was before "the Bloods" became the name of a gang, but I still didn't think it would be appropriate for me to use that term.

When school let out we were headed south again. Peter must have sold his tools because all we had were the clothes and bags on our backs again. Somehow we had a ride or enough money to get to San Luis Obispo but we would have to hitchhike the rest of the way back to L.A.

When we landed in Venice Beach, we had a trumpet player friend named Mike Kopek who had a big house that belonged to his mother. Our credit must have been good because he rented some rooms to us and I know we didn't have any money. Paris, Bigness and Tony Scott (not the saxophone player) or Joaquin Murriata as he liked to be called, were on the scene and the big house was a hangout for people like that, an interesting group of people. As a young man fairly unlearned in the ways of love and romance, I witnessed Paris' talents of seduction that he applied with barely a word. Several of us were sitting on the porch around sunset talking about everything and nothing in particular and it suddenly occurred to me that a magnetism was building between Paris and an attractive brunette sitting with us until they both seemed to be glowing. When it reached a zenith for about 2 or 3 minutes, Paris held out his hand, she put hers in his and they both walked off into the sunset holding hands in a kind of magically passionate aura that neither wanted to disturb with words.

Needless to say, I was very impressed. As a young lad of fifteen there is so much to learn. In learned and sophisticated cultures, such as the Jewish for one, though a boy is proclaimed a man at thirteen at his bar mitzvah, he is not considered to have reached adult maturity until he is thirty years old. However, there is always a lot to learn at any age. It seems the greatest learning takes place when we are receptive enough ,when a new experience presents itself. There is a tendency to give up on ourselves and adopt attitudes and dispositions that reflect that. Working a little harder, a little more intelligently, we can be ready for a new level of experience, or maybe we already are and just need to be more receptive. We are never too old or too young to push ourselves in a reasonable manner, or just be more receptive, or both.

I can't help but think that sometimes, to some degree, wisdom is wasted on the old. But that is also a fallacy. At a certain absolute level, everything is as it should be, and the greatest part of being who we are is beyond age and physical illusion. That of course is a spiritual perception, an experience beyond words or conventional thought.

At any rate, it was summer, and the place to find me would be the beach. I would walk out to the center of Venice Beach at Windward Avenue past the Pavilion out to the breakwater, as previously mentioned, and walk north along

the beach until I got to Santa Monica. On
the north side of the Santa Monica Pier, past
that breakwater, were the waves I liked the
best. One day, who should I see but some of
my old friends from Laguna Beach. They had
hitchhiked up to see a surfing movie at the
Santa Monica Civic Auditorium. After hanging
out at the beach, we wandered over to see a
friend who was going to be in the movie. He
was interesting because he was a good surfer,
but he also loved motorcycles and, in fact,
he had a beautiful black and chrome Harley
Davidson chopper that he loved to ride.

Later on we all went to the surfing movie
together and there he was, riding the nose on a
fast wave at sunset, with the sun shining through
the wave, in his tall, elegant style. Afterwards
there was a wild dance party, with a live band, at
a ballroom venue on the beach in Santa Monica.
The next day we all met at the beach and decided
to hitchhike to Laguna Beach. My friend Collin
had a hideout under his back porch, where I
could sleep.

The next day I was climbing on the rocks
along the beach and somebody yelled at me,
"Hey Pat, is that you?"

I yelled back, "Hey Bob! What's happening."

It was Bob Burton.

"I'm making the Laguna Beach scene, man!" he said looking incredulous to be seeing me.

"It's so amazing running into you here," I said.

"Come on, let me show you what I'm doing," he invited.

"Sure," I said not, having any other plans. So I followed him along to a hat shop on the South Coast Highway. It was a small space, a little bigger than Peter's gallery was when we lived in Laguna. The shop had hats of all shapes and sizes, and a wide assortment of decorations, from little beer cans to flowers and beachcomber items.

I could tell he was having fun with it and was a friend of the shop owner. "Hey, you know Jerry and Judy, our friends with the horse from Vallarta, are here," he added.

"No, I didn't know. Wow, that's great!" I replied.

"Yeah, they have a friend named Angel that runs the hamburger joint and they work there. You should go by and get something to eat. They specialize in French Fries dipped in Roquefort sauce."

So I left Bob to his hats and went in search of food. Sure enough, there was Judy flipping burgers and, after greeting each other warmly, she was more than happy to feed me. As I was eating, I looked down the beach and saw that St. Anne's, Thalia, Oak and Brook Street had beautifully breaking waves. I was lucky enough to know where I could find some fins, which you really need to catch reef breaks, and spent the rest of the day enjoying some of the best body surfing of my life.

The next day, the surf was flat again and not wanting to wear out my welcome, I decided it was time to head back north again to Venice Beach. This went on all summer long, back and forth. The last time, I started out heading south at Lincoln Blvd. just south of the marina and a woody pulled over to pick me up.

"Where're you going" a surfer with blond curly hair asked me as we drove away.

"Laguna Beach," I replied.

"You're in luck. That's where I'm going."

"Alright!" not fully believing my good luck.

In southern California, on many summer mornings, the marine cloud layer shrouds the coast and brings with it a smoky blue mist. As the sun slowly breaks, the camouflage changes, introducing a misty marble of blue, gold, and grey. We headed through the wetlands between Marina del Rey and Playa del Rey, where Howard Hughes had created aviation wonders and now where DreamWorks makes movies.

The sun was heralding a glorious day. Only the winding marshes were swaddled here and there with low banks of fog.

Smokey Blue

Alone and mystified
A smoky blue fog is cast
Over hidden realities of minds and bodies
Moving toward their destinies
As slowly as the movement of the earth
Not slow at all, at over 1000 MPH
The power of illusion
Is given poetic beauty
Under a gentle shroud of mist
Life waits to burst forth
Redefining reality
As the mind thinks it knows it
Yes, alone and mystified
A beautiful truth is waiting
To be discovered
Yet not waiting at all
A fantastic party beyond imagination
Waits inside
Those lighted windows
Lost in and beyond time
One wonders if the next car will stop
When you take a chance

Hitchhiking in paradise
The wave is poised to break out of sight
In the smoky blue
Alone and mystified.

"Laguna Beach, huh? The surf's better down that way. I'm going there to see my girlfriend Candy Calhoun."

"Candy Calhoun! Her sister Robin was my girlfriend in the eighth grade, what a coincidence," I replied.

"She's a world champion surfer, but I admire her for following her true passion, which is art. You may have heard of me, my name is Mike Doyle."

"Please to meet you, my name's Pat Krohn," I replied. "Of course I've heard of you. You won the world championship at Makaha." Mike Doyle was a regular in Surfer magazine back in the sixties.

"Yeah, but the truth is the sport I love the most is right there," he said, pointing to a pair of fins on the floor at my feet. "If I didn't have a date, we'd be stopping at the Wedge and do some body surfing." The Wedge is a spot that in those days, when the boards were bigger, could only be body surfed. On a normal day, the deep, deep swell comes up on the steep beach and the jetty with such extreme proportion that it suddenly creates a very thick, massive wave that comes crashing down with bone breaking power.

However, all of that speed and power extrapolates into an incredibly exhilarating ride, especially if a particularly large swell comes through when it peaks up into a grotesque monster with an 18 foot face (where even a 10 foot face is beyond what many experienced surfers will challenge). I, for one, after body surfing it on a normal day, prefer to simply marvel at these giant waves as a wonder of nature.

And so it went, talking about surfing or just driving along in silence, enjoying the ride in the finest woody on the planet. When I made the sojourn to Laguna, all I had was a Hawaiian shirt, a pair of jeans, a pair of low-top converse sneakers that Phyllis Dillon had bought me, a corduroy sports coat, a bathing suit hanging out of my back pocket, and no money at all.

First I thought I'd go to the hat shop and see if Bob Burton was there, which he wasn't, but there was a very nice lady who told me where I could find him. "Just go to Victoria Cove. He's in that big house on the left when you get to the first stop sign down off the highway." That was about a three-mile walk down the highway, but that was okay with me. I did a lot of walking in those days. When I got there, Bob, as always, was glad to see me, which I always got a kick out of. The whole gang was there; Jerry and Judy and a new person, Donna Glider, a very sweet, gentle person who would become a good friend to me, but who was very sad because her boyfriend had just been busted for pot possession.

"You'll never guess what we have!" Bob teased me.

"Tell me what" I said. "We just got a big box of peyote buttons from the Native American Church," he replied.

"Wow, that's really great. Ever since that great contact high I got from you guys in Sarasota, I've wanted to see what the real thing was like," I said expressing my delight.

"We're really glad you came. We're leaving for a week to Mexico and you can stay here while we're gone." He showed me where the peyote was and there was a genuine Hobey surfboard I could use too. I said thanks and that I was really looking forward to surfing and taking some peyote.

The next morning I got up early and took the board up on the highway and hitched a ride to Doheny State Park to catch some waves. That was supposed to be a good place to learn how to surf. I paddled out and the main problem I had was watching for other surfers. After a couple hours of halfway riding waves, I figured that was enough for one day and vowed to come back soon and get good at it.

Later on that afternoon, I ran into my friend Collin who said he had a job for me at Old Brussels restaurant washing dishes. I spent the next three days working at night and hanging out at the beach during the day with my friends. Surfing was too much like work, but body surfing felt much more natural for me.

Friday night there was going to be a dance, but I wanted to try the peyote, so I thought, "If I feel like going to the dance after I've eaten eight buttons of peyote, I'll go. Otherwise I'll just enjoy the night." So I sat on a comfortable chair, made a cup of Jasmine tea and broke up the buttons into small pill-size pieces (it was dry and brittle) and swallowed a couple and drank some tea. Peyote is one of the worst tasting things you can eat. I made it through about six buttons and then just sat there enjoying the sunset and not feeling anything in particular. I thought, "The dance will be starting soon, I guess I'll head down there." On the way, I gradually noticed my senses seemed to be keener and I thought, "This must be what it felt like to be an American native before the pollution of the white man," as if one could simply ingest even a natural substance and create that consciousness. Nevertheless, that was my perception, however valid or invalid.

When I got to the dance it was just getting started. No one was dancing as the band was just getting set up. By the time they started playing the hall was half full. It was a surfer band playing Dick Dale style. He was the creator of that style, pre-empting the Beach Boys who were smoother and not nearly as radical. Everybody was doing the Surfer Stomp. The legs pump to a flat footed or heel oriented stomping to a very strong, almost tribal rock beat, allowing for a lot of improvisation mimicking a walk to the nose of a big surfboard as was used then, or whatever fancy came to mind. It followed the trend of not holding your partner's hand, but you could do that if you wanted. It was really quite erotic the way the girls did it with all the pumping of the legs and so forth, to the very strong almost primitive rock beat, and with a hundred sexually driven young people all wildly stomping it seemed like some kind of tribal summer solstice erotic rite. A friend had a fifth of whisky he shared with me which smoothed and helped sensualize the intense feelings that were being amplified by the peyote.

I stepped out for a few minutes on a small deck area out one of the side doors. It was a pleasant balmy summer night, the stars were performing a concert of twinkles and Venus was the star of the show with its multi-colored prismatic effect. The breeze felt pleasantly cool and the blackness of the night seemed intoxicating, but the dancing bodies inside writhing with pleasure and jubilation beckoned me once more and so the night went.

On the way home, a couple of girls I knew were talking and one of them seemed to give me a very warm greeting. I was feeling very uninhibited and she seemed to be very receptive. In a moment, my lips were touching hers and sensually discovering what it felt like to be kissing her. The beautiful thing about young love is that you know that your partner or you are probably not ready for anything more than a kiss, so a kiss alone is an exquisite experience that you savor and I kissed a lot of pretty young lips. I don't remember any plain ones.

As I proceeded home under that particular magic spell, I was thinking how lucky I was to be alive. With all my freedom and a great pad at my disposal, I was beginning to feel kind of adult and sophisticated, although I didn't really know what that meant. It fostered fantasies, possibly engendered by Frank Sinatra movies or such, of having a quiet party with a few girls and a couple of other guys, a certain amount of alcohol content, some mood music, and whatever else the imagination would allow.

I wasn't really in circulation and was out of touch with what was in and who was who. I had a friend named Kenny Davis, who I regarded as the man about town, sort of the surfer equivalent of "the Fonz." I knew I would find him on the beach at Thalia Street surrounded by pretty girls in two-piece bathing suits. Sure enough, I was right.

"Hey Kenny, how's it going?" I ventured as I sat on a rock nearby.

"Beautiful day, but no waves man," Kenny answered. "By the way, I thought it was kind of weird the way you were dancing last night, but the chicks dug it," he said. Kenny and I had been on the same Babe Ruth League team back in the eighth grade and I enjoyed the fact that he found me amusing.

"Guess what, I've got this great pad all to myself and it's really nice. I was thinking it would be perfect if a few of us guys and a few girls had a little party there tonight," I suggested.

Kenny was not one to make quick decisions so he said, "I'd like to check out your scene. I'll get back to you in about an hour; I think we can make this happen."

I stayed at the Beach and played in the shore break and lay on the beach until he got back.   "Alright, it's on. Me and John and our girls and this other girl that's really fine – she says she's crazy about you, maybe you know her. Her name's Carol," Ken said with an air of satisfaction and a happy look on his face.

"You mean that foxy looking chick with the Sophia Loren body and Elizabeth Taylor face I met on the beach yesterday?"

"That's the one. I like the way you exaggerate."

I went home and did my best to make everything inviting. Ken and his girl came with a bottle of Bacardi and John and his girl came with a bottle of Cutty Sark Scotch. Carol brought cokes, ginger ale and ice and the refreshments were set. We made ourselves comfortable and after a few drinks started making out.

Somehow word had gotten out that there was a big surfer party on Victoria Street. We wouldn't let anybody in so they started partying on the lawn. This caused a big scene and somebody called the cops. The next thing I knew Carol and I were running out the back after somebody yelled, "The cops are here! The cops are here!" Carol and I ran down the street leading to the beach. "Don't worry; I'll get you home so you don't get in trouble. Let's go along the beach until we get to Agate Street," I assured her, really worried about getting in trouble myself and being thrown in jail and "Juvie." We were all under age and there was a lot of booze on the premises. I helped her get up on the rocks and whenever she needed help getting up or down, which was all pretty exciting and sexy because she was so beautiful with long legs, beautiful thighs and breasts and face and she was lightly clad in shorts. It was probably a good thing the cops came. Meanwhile we were climbing on rocks, getting splashed by waves and making our way slowly down the beach. I was surprised how well she did. We finally got to Agate Street and followed the streets home to her house, kissed, and said our good-byes, never to see each other again.

I decided the only thing for me to do was crash under Collins's porch. Early the next morning, Collin said "Pat! What are you doing here?"

"Well I had to hide out and crash somewhere," I replied.

"Yeah, I heard about the party. Hey, the cops are looking for you. You'd better skip town."

When I got home to Venice Beach, the house

was a mess and when Peter and Jean came home they said, "Look boys, we're profoundly tired from all the struggling and we're taking a break." Peter was now 39 and Jean was 37. When you're young, strong, talented and beautiful, people always seem to be glad to see you and you get any job you apply for, capabilities and opportunities abound, but when you start closing in on your forties, people expect you to be established.

The fact that Peter and Jean were always fighting indicated that what was once a living dream without end, was in fact ending. The next nine months was a period of them breaking up, then briefly making up again, and then permanently breaking up. So ended what I call the Krohnicles, our time together as Krohns and apart from the mainstream.

The good news is that we all survived this by going our own ways. No matter how good your intentions and ideals are, unless a family unit can come together and make things work together, people must go their own ways. During this period Peter said to me, "You know, Pat, the only truth is constant doubt."

"What do you mean?" I asked him. "Nothing stays the same, everything changes. Always question what is happening today, because everything becomes something else tomorrow, and even from moment to moment, Hence constant doubt."

When people become extremely intellectual, they become concerned only with tangible truth. The most important values I had experienced in my 15 years of life as a Krohn, were love, loyalty, goodness, kindness, hopes, dreams, wonder and imagination which were all basically and essentially intangible at the intellectual level until they become linked to the intellect. That's when we forget their intangible nature, because in this world we are ruled by the mind, which should be working for the soul, which is intangible. Those paramount qualities of the soul, like what makes people experience love, should be ruling the mind. To discover and learn how is the spiritual quest, but I was too young then, and perhaps even now, to convince anyone of that. However, there is wisdom in constant doubt, in the absence of knowing how to make the mind work for the soul, which is probably why a great teacher once said, "Be as cautious as a serpent and as innocent as a dove."

Maybe the Krohnicles come to an end too soon, but nothing really ends, it just changes. Peter soon starts a new family and goes on to many other and perhaps even greater artistic achievements. Jean continues to write prose and poetry and goes to UCLA to get a bachelor's degree in English. Lee stays with Jean for another year or so, but eventually must find his own way as well. We boys all find ways to express our artistic natures and got on with lives immeasurably imbued by the life we lived when we were all together. To this day we remain personally connected.

As a young man of fifteen, both uniquely prepared and unprepared, I became responsible for my own life, which became a new story in the adult bohemian and conventional worlds of jazz, art, gardening, family, pre-hippy, hippy, travel, cars, natural foods, dancing, Viet Nam War draft, and spiritual pursuits. Someday I will endeavor to write about these and the people and places who enriched and influenced my life along the way in the quest for the understanding of what it means to be human.

After Thoughts

Rather than fiction, which is a creation, this story is a reflection of people, places and things that *were* and *are*. The main characters are my mother, my father, my brothers, and myself. More of it seems to be about me than about my father, mother, and my brothers. But this is one of the great misunderstandings of life. Roles are defined by what people do for the most part. How these roles are played out tells a story. Those things that happen "to," "by," and "for" the people in those roles have an aspect that can be told in words, and another much larger aspect that words are quite useless to express, because the real things like true love are beyond words, preconceived notions, or concepts of any kind. A person's story has all the people in it that entered that story and it tells that part of them.

Many years ago in a book by Eric Fromm, I read about the art of loving. He writes about unconditional love and how it epitomizes our mother's love. This humble kind of love is an extension of the infinite love that permeates all being and is in fact the Supreme Being. The relationship between that and a father's love can perhaps, at least partially, be understood by a sapphire or a turquoise stone in its matrix. By itself the stone is cold and lonely compared to the way it looks in the matrix. When the matrix still has the stone in its midst, it takes on a beauty far beyond its earthy makeup, and in some ways, as in the story that is told by its hued and hewn textures, and fine schisms and colors, is even more beautiful than the stone. However, the definable actions, which tell the story, are created by the stone. In truth, spiritual beings that are having a human experience are not easily definable, and psyches are beyond male and female definition. This illustration is overly simplified. Sometimes Jean was the stone and Peter was the matrix, and sometimes they were both aspects of both at the same time, and in truth perhaps always. Another perception, brought up by my friend Ellie, is that I am the jewel in the story, since it's my story and most of the thoughts and feelings expressed are my own, my family is the matrix. So many perceptions are beholding the truth in a different way.

Peter was my father; Jean was my mother, but what about the parent of that other self? The self that, is always silent, always aware, and says, "I experienced that." The source of existence, which is the parent of that, self, is perhaps beyond what we can conceive of as a mother or a father. Just as the drop is unqualified to write about the ocean, I am unqualified to write about that greatest of all sources. However, just as a child waits to grow up, this drop endeavors to become that ocean.

Jean, in my mind has always been the family leader and example of unconditional love. Getting recognition for her writing and poetry even in the bohemian world in those days was almost impossible, and because of her Catholic upbringing it was easy for her to focus more on Peter's efforts and help him. That's the way it was. Jean never really got the full credit for her part in so many creative things they both did together, and she summed it up in a poem.

No Fame, No Blame, No Shame

There is no fame,
There is no blame,
There is no shame,
There just is.

Perhaps more details could have been provided, more "fleshing out" could have been done. Please understand that my parents were

Zen Buddhists and I was avoiding clichés. This life that we are living is the ongoing culmination of the history of mankind. This is, I hope, my unique statement of the first fifteen years of my life in a family fully conscious of being purposefully unlike any other.

Made in the USA
Charleston, SC
21 March 2013